GW01339657

Howard Firby on

SWIMMING

Howard Firby on
SWIMMING

PELHAM BOOKS

First published in Great Britain by Pelham Books Ltd
52 Bedford Square, London WC1B 3EF
1975

© 1975 by Howard Firby

All Rights Reserved. No part of this publication
may be reproduced, stored in a retrieval system,
or transmitted, in any form or by any means,
electronic, mechanical, photocopying, recording
or otherwise, without the prior permission of the
Copyright owner.

ISBN 0 7207 0762 5

Set and printed in Great Britain by
Western Printing Services Ltd, Bristol
in Caledonia ten on twelve point and bound by
James Burn, Esher, Surrey

CONTENTS

	Introduction	7
1	Feel of the water	13
2	Freestyle	20
3	Backstroke	46
4	Breaststroke	62
5	Butterfly	87
6	Wave patterns	110
7	Starts and turns	121

Introduction

You are bound to notice in this book that at almost every juncture I have viewed some aspect of swimming in a unique way. It's reasonable, therefore, that I introduce myself and offer some insight into my background. I should also explain in a general way my philosophy on the sport.

For more than 27 years now I have been a swimming coach. For most of those years I was strictly amateur but later I became a full-time professional. I have coached at all levels from age-group novice through to Olympic team.

Note that I said "coach" and not "instructor". From the beginning I have been singlemindedly concerned with the coaching of swimmers to go faster. Just as a professor of English may be fascinated by the subtleties of the language without ever being expected to teach a child to read, I have never found myself in the situation of teaching a non-swimmer to swim.

Shortly after the Second World War, I started my coaching with a handful of teenagers—I was 22 myself—in a 13-yard, 3-lane, 40-year-old dungeon of a "Y" pool in Regina, Saskatchewan, a city on the Canadian prairies which was then small and remote. It was especially remote in terms of swimming background and interest. There was no competitive swimming of worth within perhaps a thousand miles, and hardly any within two hundred.

I was obliged from the start to educate myself in everything to do with the sport. Although I had been a "strong swimmer" and a lifeguard in my teens, I had never been a competitive swimmer. I had never even heard of the Canadian Amateur Swimming Association until I found myself in coaching.

I had to start from scratch as a "Head Coach" (only coach in my case) knowing virtually nothing about training or the strokes. I didn't even know the rules. (Twenty-two years later, as

C.A.S.A.'s Rules Chairman, I literally rewrote the Association's Swimming Rules.) All I had was an insatiable curiosity and an open mind. I couldn't know at the time what an advantage I had to be able to start in that way, more or less unencumbered by the dogmatisms that plagued—and still plague—swimming.

I took that freethinker's approach with me when I went on to coach three of Canada's largest and most successful clubs.

More recently I was the full-time National Technical Director/Advisor of the Canadian Amateur Swimming Association. In that job I travelled all over Canada visiting clubs. In so-doing, the best-received of my offerings were in the fields of stroke coaching (technique), "poolside manner", and workout orchestration.

As both coach and guest coach I have worked with large and small squads of swimmers at every level of ability under all sorts of conditions and in virtually every size and description of pool, from a shipboard pool five yards by seven (a "Games" team crossing the Atlantic) to a pool 220 yards in length (with the aid of binoculars).

Swimming "trips" have taken me throughout the world. I've observed and absorbed, and originated a wide range of stroke improvement drills, coaching gimmicks, and other tricks of the trade.

At the end of the Second World War, I spent nearly a year in a military orthopaedic hospital as a victim of polio. Formerly a good track athlete, I literally went through the process of learning to walk again (I still carry a cane at times).

As part of my therapy I was exposed to the study of human physiology. It became of vital interest to me, especially that part which deals with muscles and how they work. That study, which is still going on, came easily to me because I have always been able to draw. Earlier, as an avid teenage designer and builder of model airplanes, and then as an air force pilot, I had been steeped in the physics of aerodynamics and in the closely related subject of hydrodynamics.

All along in my coaching I have applied my knowledge in these areas—hydrodynamics, human physiology, etc. In a very real sense my swimmers have been *models* I have shaped and then let loose at meets, just as my model airplanes had been earlier. Even today, as much as I enjoy the human relationships of coaching, whenever I observe a swimmer in action I can't help seeing

INTRODUCTION

design shapes, wave patterns, laminar-flow phenomena, and the like.

The observations and theories I give in this book stem from my long interest in the achieving of the best-possible combinations of streamlining and delivered power. As I see it, a swimming coach faces a challenge not encountered by, say, a rowing coach. The rowing coach orders his boats from others—master designers-builders—and concentrates his own efforts on the training of his crews. In swimming, each athlete is in a sense his own boat, so the swimming coach must—or should—shape his boats *and* train their one-man crews at one and the same time. In so-doing, the knowledgeable swimming coach will often compromise power for the sake of better streamlining and, vice versa, "buy" some drag in order to achieve more power, always working within the confines of the immutable laws of fluid mechanics and keeping in mind the physical and mental resources embodied in each of his swimmers.

I'm convinced that the majority of swimmers work much harder in competition than they need to for the results they get. Losers often expend more effort than winners. It is not uncommon for a swimmer to work long and hard over a period of months in the hope of improving his time by a few seconds, an improvement he might have realized in just a few days with minor adjustments in his technique.

An analogy is as follows: With a sledge-hammer and a lot of whacking it is possible to fell a large tree, splinters can be mashed and bashed off until eventually the tree will fall over; but a lumberjack in a chopping contest would not dream of using such a crude instrument.

In the same vein it is puzzling that so many of the same coaches who have their swimmers "shave down" (shave the hair from their legs, arms, and chest to reduce drag) before a race can blithely ignore other, more important aspects of streamlining in their daily indifference to stroke refinement.

These same coaches often herd their swimmers through 1,500 and more miles a season—in two seasons the width of the Atlantic! If these coaches were to contemplate personally rowing an equivalent distance I am sure they would select their boats and oars with more thought given to efficiency of design than they offer their swimmers.

My references to boats are perhaps unfortunate. Our bodies are not like boats, and when we swim our propelling movements are more sophisticated than those used in rowing or paddling.

The main difference is that we swim *through* the water, not along it or over it. Our specific gravity is such that we float normally with 49/50ths of our mass submerged—even icebergs do better.

And we don't hydroplane! The fastest swimming speed ever attained in competition (4.89 m.p.h. by Steve Clarke in a 50-yard freestyle race, according to the *1974 Guinness Book of Records*) is nowhere near the necessary speed for hydroplaning (about 15 m.p.h.). We simply cannot hydroplane under our own power, no matter what many outstanding swimmers have felt they were doing. This "old wives' tale" about hydroplaning is only one of the many misconceptions which riddle the sport.

That there were—and still are—so many misconceptions is probably due to Man's long association with boats and to his traditional apprehension of bodies of water and their murky depths. (Did you know that only about one hundred years ago there were still countries with laws *against* attempting to rescue drowning persons?; the Deity's will, or some such superstition.)

There is no doubt that we are still emerging from what might be called "The Dark Ages of Swimming". Unfortunately, some four decades ago the process was set back by a coterie of well-meaning but uninformed well-known coaches around the world. These "experts", upon finding themselves in the then-new limelight of media attention and public acclaim—acclaim based largely on curiosity, ignorance, and a wonderment that *anyone could swim* so well and *so far*—came out with all sorts of quaint notions about swimming methods that were eagerly accepted as "gospel". These *gurus* of early organized swimming—who knew less about sound swimming technique than your average age-grouper of today—"spoke" and the throng "believed".

Most of their erroneous dogmatisms have now been discarded by those in the inner circle of serious, world-class coaching. But the damage was done: Armies of sincere "instructors" as well as the typical "go by the manual" learn-to-swim programmes still revere and teach many of the old misguided concepts.

And it's not only the "instructors". Even today there are well-known coaching authorities who apparently see only what they want to believe when analysing stroke technique—even if it isn't there to be seen. Time and again I have heard such authorities on the sound-tracks of films describing "key features" of a swimmer's stroke when it is obvious that the swimmer in question on the film, who often is in fact a pupil of the commentating coach, is doing something quite different. The "authority" may say, for example: "Of course there is a strong push back to full extension in the butterfly arm stroke", when on the screen it is startlingly clear that the star swimmer is pushing back only as far as the mid-point of the hips before lifting his hands out into the recovery.

There are altogether too many "of courses" thrown around indiscriminately by persons who should know better: "*Of course* it's wrong to arch the back in breaststroke" (many of the world's best do); "*of course* it's best to keep the hips level in freestyle . . . to prevent the rolling" (not one world-ranked swimmer does; and so on).

The rewards are great for the coach who opens his eyes, who allows himself to learn *from* his best swimmers, who puts each of the often-parrotted dictums on stroke technique to the test of critical inspection. He will be astonished at how many of his preconceived and cherished notions simply are not as plausible as they once seemed. The best swimmers, the ones who have logged the miles and the years, and who have unwittingly transcended their coaches' faulty understanding of technique, have all along been ahead of most of the blindly-accepted pontifications. For example; one of the legendary names in coaching, Robert Kiphuth, in his 1942 book *Swimming*, expounded vigorously on the absolute necessity of keeping the body shoulders-level flat in freestyle, yet, on the dust jacket of the book, and in his freestyle chapter, he featured a large, spectacular photograph of one of his best swimmers *rolled completely to one side* spearing along through the water in the manner of the current champions. Another example, Hungarian authority, Bela Rajki, in his 1956 book *The Technique of Competitive Swimming*, commented on a sequence of underwater photographs of the 1952 Olympic sprint champion to the effect that *in spite* of her rolling her technique was successful—it would seem that she won in spite of her coaching, and so it has been all along. The truths have been obvious while the coaching fraternity has tended to stick with, and even add to, the cluster of unfounded theorums.

But take heart! More-learned aquatic experts have been wrong. Naval designers faced with the problem of shaping the first nuclear-powered submarines—which would differ from the then-conventional submarines in as much that they would spend most of their time at sea submerged—experimented and came up with the now-familiar whale-shape configuration. (The design, by Mother Nature, had been there, waiting to be appreciated, through countless millennia.) A half-scale pilot model, powered by the diesel engines of the day, was built to test the new design at sea. Can you imagine the "if only we'd known" shock and amazement of the admirals who had just come through a bitter undersea war, when the test submarine proved to be faster (speed classified) than their surface warships?

Note that it wasn't superior horsepower that made it possible; it was simply a matter of better designing to fit the water. In a manner of speaking, the designers merely gave the new submarine *better technique*.

Although I recognize that I am a "technique oriented coach", I am among the first to agree that superior technique by itself cannot make champions. It plays only a small but essential part in the achieving of success. I know that little gold stars are not affixed to a swimmer's time card for "style". Winning is the objective. But style can be vital to the process.

Efficient technique should be acquired early in a swimmer's career so he can get on with being an athlete—an athlete who just happens to do his competing as a swimmer—which is what the sport is all about.

In the ensuing chapters I will attempt to show how easy it is to give these swimming athletes the skills they need. I will acquaint you with a wide variety of proven instructional "gimmicks" and general tips that can make any coach more confident, and therefore more proficient, on his own pool deck.

CHAPTER 1

Feel of the Water

In coaching circles the expression "feel of the water" is common. It's used when discussing that "something extra" which some swimmers have going for them which enables them to move through the water with seeming ease while others struggle. It's often shortened to simply "feel".

Swimmers with *feel* exhibit an uncanny ability to always align themselves in the water, the better to slither-slink along. And unlike the strugglers, they somehow "know" when and where and at what rate to exert force as they propel themselves along.

The tendency is to think of *feel* only in terms of "educated hands". (Lecturing coaches at competitive swimming forums when commenting on *feel* invariably hold out a hand to duplicate in the air the beginning motions of a pull.) But *feel* is more than an acute sensitivity of the hands; it's a total thing, involving the entire body. Internally, it amounts to a responsive awareness of the efficient use of one's muscles and levers. Externally, it is a computer-quick cognizance of, and reaction to, the most minute variations in pressure on the skin surfaces of the body—like being sunburnt all over.

Storybook safe-crackers sandpaper their fingertips, the better to *feel* out the elusive combinations. I don't suggest that swimmers use sandpaper—although I have heard of some who did—but it's worth noting that some claim they *feel the water* with a new awareness when they have shaved down for competition.

The popular belief seems to be that a small percentage of swimmers are blessed with *feel* while most are not, and that there is nothing much a coach can do about it except rejoice when he finds a "natural" in one of his groups.

I cannot accept that premise. I'm convinced that most individuals start out with a considerable degree of latent *feel* which all too often is maimed into disuse by instructional methods better suited to the programming of robots. I believe that *feel* can be developed through the use of sound teaching-learning methods.

It's been said that we humans have not truly learned something—we don't "own" a skill—until we have virtually forgotten how and when we learned it. Our command of a skill, be it the speaking of another language, the catching of a ball, or the performing of a swimming stroke, is not truly complete until it has become "second nature" to us. Learned *feel* can become *second nature* to most swimmers when "natural" learning is encouraged.

We learn best when we teach ourselves. The teacher may direct the course of instruction but in the final analysis we take what is taught and recode it to suit our own memory-bank and file it away, *i.e.*, we *learn* it. That done, it is more likely to be retained and to manifest itself as second nature. The process is especially true in the acquiring of motor skills: We may be shown how, but *we learn by doing*, *i.e.* through experience.

A practical application of this is the use of stroke drills designed to encourage the novice swimmer to discover *for himself* the subtleties of the desired techniques.

Do not misunderstand me. I am not suggesting that we coaches should allow our swimmers to swim "any old way". Far from it. I'm saying that we should take steps to devise, and use, teaching (learning) drills which will forcefully nudge our charges toward learning for themselves the specific natural movements we know to be the most efficient and successful.

These natural movements need not even be mentioned in the coach's explanation of each new drill. For example, it's possible—ridiculously easy in fact—for a coach to shift most of a squad from a plodding, mechanically-inept freestyle to the slinky *feel*-charged stroke of Mark Spitz in only one session without once mentioning the bent-arm pull, the timing of the pulls, or the overall timing of the stroke. The swimmers may not retain the new stroke in competition after only one session—that may take a few weeks—but at least they experience it and recognize its advantages after only one session, depending on the coach's skill in the use of descriptive word-pictures. (Too few coaches bother to acquire a spell-binding ability to sell the pure joy of swimming itself.) This *feel* for freestyle can be nurtured into life by, of all things, the use of "dogpaddle" (as I will explain in my freestyle chapter).

Virtually any aspect of swimming technique can be implanted through the intelligent use of stroke drills. The coach remains in charge; he directs, supervises, and monitors the learning sessions, bringing off a good portion of his stroke-improvement results indirectly.

Those coaches who equate "stroke work" with time-out from serious training—and many in my experience seem to think that way—should learn that almost every form of stroke-improvement drill can be made to blend into the main body of a hard workout. Once the swimmers are familiar with a drill, they can do it "against time" according to any hard interval training pattern favoured by the imaginative coach.

Take "fist swimming" as an example. The swimmers merely close their fists as they otherwise swim normally. This simple alteration develops the *feel* of pulling not only with the hands but with the forearms as well. To pull effectively while the fists are closed, the swimmer must instinctively seek out the movements of the classic bent-arm pull, no matter which stroke. "Dropped elbows" in freestyle correct themselves, the "over the barrel" feeling of the pull is induced, and ineffectual prettinesses are suppressed. Once mastered, fist swimming is not significantly slower than full-stroke swimming, nor should it be, the total area of the pulling surfaces is only slightly reduced. There is, however, some loss of the use of the hands as sculling blades.

As with most drill strokes, fist swimming can lend variety and zest to offset the all-too-prevalent boredom of day-in-day-out training. It may be done: (1) in straight sets of interval-training swims; (2) in the first half (or part) of each repeat (the remainder of the repeat to be done hands-open); (3) in every other repeat swim of a set; (4) in alternate lengths of longer swims; (5) in the first half of each length (great for sprinters on short, fast swims); (6) in "wind sprints" (*i.e.* short, full-speed sprints of, say, 25 metres while holding the breath); (7) in individual medley repeats; (8) in arms-only swims (a real test); (9) when warming up (as a regular routine prior to workouts); and so on. It blends in so well, in fact, that a casual observer may not notice it.

My long experience with the use of stroke drills—I think I have always used them—has been that when teaching a group a new drill it is best to first carefully explain what you want, then set the group going on the drill in the water, call them out after a few minutes and have one or two who were doing it well (preferably *not* the usual stars of the squad) act as demonstrators as you go through the explanation again, then set the group going again for perhaps 10 minutes at the most—more than that goes against what is known about how we learn best—in many short exposures. The first day with a new drill, perhaps 8 in a group of 35 will pick it up reasonably well. The second time around, in a subsequent session, with the help of demonstrators and another careful explanation, another 6 to 10 will get the hang of it. The third exposure may bring the total to, say, 25. And so on until all but a handful have grasped it. With the remainder, you may have to resort to personalized, one-to-one coaching.

In a few months, the group can own a considerable repertoire of drills for each of the strokes. Then the concocting of productive and *interesting* workouts on short notice is easy.

I have found it useful to give easily-remembered names to the various drills. This saves time in orchestrating workouts. The coach has merely to come out with: "Okay, next, let's do a 'dirty thirty', 'fist swimming' every other repeat, on a pace time of . . ."

When I have noticed my group exhibiting a particular weakness at a meet (it is easier to spot such common-to-the-group deficiencies when seen against, and compared to, an unfamiliar norm) I have devised new corrective drills, or resurrected old ones, for use during the following weeks until the flaw is overcome.

Veteran swimmers as well as novices profit from the regular use of stroke drills. It's not at all uncommon, for example, to see Olympic swimmers using, and enjoying, their pet drills when working out in the Olympic pool. In time, the coach will know which drills work best on which swimmers in his top group.

The proficient coach will use any and all methods that get results. I use a poolside blackboard for group and individual chalk-talks (it helps to be able to draw); I use plasticine (clay) to model dolphins, legs, arms, the complete human form (it is my favourite teaching tool, I can shape it into any position, and even distort it —add a dorsal fin to the hips for butterfly, for example—to show virtually any aspect of good or bad technique); I use stroke sequence photos taken from swimming magazines (mounted under plastic and kept in ring-binders for poolside use); I use commercially-produced stroke films; I use stroke charts (my own, mostly); I use my own Super-8 movies; I use dryland drills, and so on. In technique coaching, the results justify the means.

"If the learner hasn't learned, the teacher hasn't taught" is a good maxim to coach by.

I reiterate that that elusive special dimension of swimming known as *feel* can be nurtured in nearly all individuals, *i.e.*, it can be learned. *Feel* is *not* rare. It has simply been overlooked or unwittingly suppressed by the majority of coaches who in their insecure knowledge of the subtleties of technique approach the teaching of strokes as a sergeant might approach rifle drill—"by the numbers". As a former freelance commercial artist of some twenty years' experience, and as a one-time art school teacher, I can state that the familiar "paint by numbers" kits tend to stifle rather than help the development of true creative skills. It's unfortunate but this same sort of unimaginative methodology still pervades most swimming instruction: "do this", "push this far", "bend here", and so on—*by the numbers, two, three, four*. The result is that in the sport there are countless so-called competitors who are, for the most part, mechanical robots and no match for the few with *feel* or, if you like, "soul".

I have gone on at some length on *feel* as it pertains to swimmers, but coaches, too, should have *feel*. Coaches who would teach *feel* must themselves have *feel*—a *feel* for *feel*, as it were.

By that I mean that the dedicated coach should strive to surmount the *by-the-numbers* barrier; he should look for the symphony of movement that is great stroke technique; he should learn to think in terms of moving body masses, momentums, clean alignments, shifting forces, and subtle nuances of timing. He should be able to see all of the above within a framework of fluid mechanics, kinesiology, physiology, and psychology—especially psychology because *feel* is a total experience in which the temperament of the individual swimmers must be taken into account. Just as music is more than so many notes strung together, so is inspired swimming more than so many levers and units of force. In other words, the coach should strive to be more than a mere craftsman, he should aspire to being an artist in the classic sense of the word. In a manner of speaking, his swimmers should be his works of art.

It takes time in the sport to understand this. The process can be speeded up, however, if the would-be coach will only open his eyes. He should study and evaluate *for himself* the techniques of the great swimmers, past and present, looking always beyond the superficial details to absorb and, in a sense, *live* the rhythms, etc. —the very essence of what he perceives.

The coach who is caught up in the daily routine of coaching—which can be repititious in the extreme—should from time to time renew his love affair with swimming. He should himself swim, at least occasionally, and he should constantly imagine the feel of the movements he teaches.

A trick I have borrowed from my years in commercial art is to look at the "artwork", *i.e.* the swimmers, upside down. Artists will turn their work upside down or look at it in a mirror to get a fresh, stranger's-eye, critical view of it now and then as they develop it. To achieve the same end while coaching, I sometimes bend over and invert my head, eyes lower than my nose. The effect is astounding! The swimmers appear to be swimming across the ceiling! Their every movement springs into focus. Stroke irregularities which had gone unnoticed before, moments of excessive drag, and the phenomena of waves and swirling water all fairly cry out for attention. So spectacular is it that I often have my pupils take turns standing on the deck at the side of the pool with their heads bent down, upside down, watching their teammates swim. I find this especially helpful in selling the porpoise-like action of good butterfly to those who are too inhibited in their own rigid version of the stroke.

This inverted "look-see" is certain to help a doubting coach appreciate the flowing, non-mechanical essence of good swimming.

Further, the coach who would understand *feel* should at every opportunity look long and hard at fishes and other creatures which are "at home" in "Mother Water". Even where there are no large aquariums there are television programmes with scenes showing dolphins, sharks, seals, and the like, swimming. Only recently, for example, I saw swimming polar bears on television filmed from below the surface—it was clear that they are fine natural swimmers and that they trail their hind legs in what modern coaches refer to as a "drag kick".

Feel is what makes the best swimmers such a joy to coach, and *the giving of this extra dimension to swimmers* who would be written-off as "ordinary" by most coaches is an even more satisfying experience.

The swimmer who knows the *feel* of his stroke when it is going well can usually detect encroaching errors early and correct them himself or seek help before things become seriously out of adjustment.

For many years now, I have encouraged each of my swimmers to think of himself as an assistant coach in charge of one swimmer —himself. This approach has produced some remarkably independent and successful athletes who, along with their *feel of the water*, have a special, even reverant, feeling for the sport, it has become their sport to enjoy.

CHAPTER 2

Freestyle

Over the years, the tendency has been to think of the freestyle stroke—or "front crawl"—as having a front end that pulls and a back end that pushes, both connected to a neutral middle section that is stable in the water, raft-like.

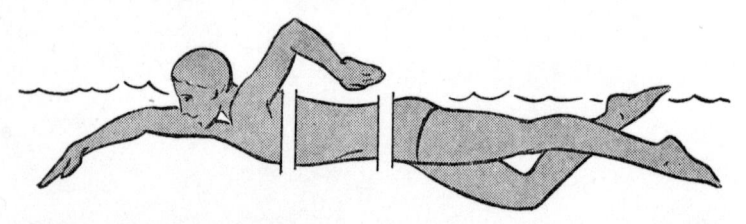

For decades there was even an emphasis on the use of what the coaching fraternity called the "independent leg drive" in which there was no set number of flutterkicks in relationship to the arm stroke cycle. The two departments were encouraged to function independently.

The stroke still suffers from over-simplified reasoning of this type.

To properly understand the way the components of the stroke

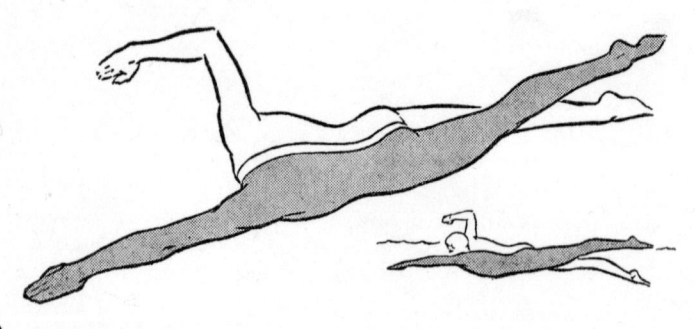

work to form the whole, it is better to imagine the body divided lengthwise into two streamlinable shapes.

With these two halves in mind, think not of one, but two "body positions" used alternately, a right-side-lined-up position and then a left-side-lined-up position. The movements of the arms and legs can then be seen to function as integral parts of the total, unit-like stroke.

Imagine that a good freestyler has in some way been coloured so that the entire left side of his body (excluding the head) is, say, red, and his right side is green. Now, if we were to take a still picture of his stroke with a camera filtered to photograph only red, we could get a picture something like this:

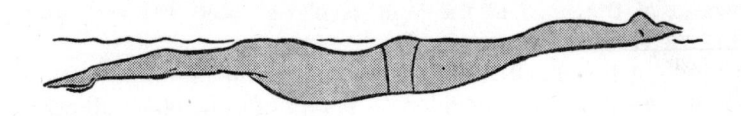

(Note that the shape is lined up from the hand to the foot—it could be a picture of a racing dive, in fact.)

If we were to take another picture through the same filter we might this time get a picture like this:

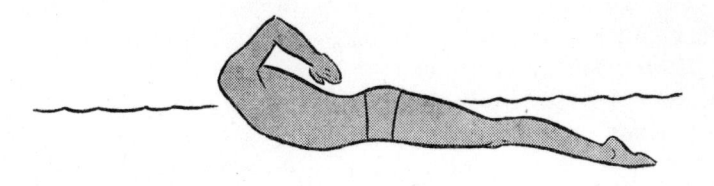

(Same side of the swimmer but caught at another point in his stroke cycle.)

But, if we had forgotten to advance the film and had therefore taken a "double exposure", the result could be a picture of the two *separate* body-halves superimposed, looking remarkably like a *complete* swimmer (minus the head) in the fact of doing well-timed freestyle. So we see it is valid to visualize the stroke as being composed of two streamlinable body halves.

Further, if we were to take a movie sequence through the same filter, the body-half would appear to be doing a stroke a lot like butterfly. (You may verify this by making a tracing of any of my illustrated freestyle stroke sequences, outlining, or filling in, only one side of the swimmer in each figure.)

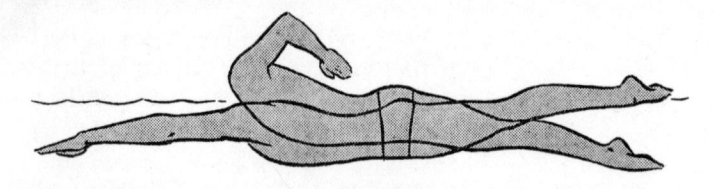

When I look at a good freestyler in action I see two half-swimmers fused together, each doing a form of butterfly out-of-phase with the other, as it were.

The up and down movements of the shoulders, and to a lesser extent of the hips, of the "out of phase" body-halves manifest themselves as a rolling action.

Rolling is a healthy feature which should be encouraged, no matter what many misguided "experts" still preach. It allows the arms to recover over the water with less strain; it positions each shoulder, in turn, for the delivering of more powerful pulls; it permits easier breathing (to the side); and best of all, it reduces drag significantly when the overall timing and alignments are right. (The body on its side, splitting the water as a ship does, has an advantage, drag is reduced by as much as one-third—which, by the way, is why we disqualify breaststrokers who swim with one shoulder lower than the other.)

Leg action

Since each leg is an integral part of its body-half, the timing of the leg action is crucial. Happily, this poses no serious problems; the act of allowing the hips to roll in time with the pivoting up and down of the shoulders influences the timing of the key, streamlined positionings of the legs.

"But", one might say, "what about the fact that many of the best freestylers use seemingly unrelated kicking tempos, such as 'two-beat', 'four-beat', 'six-beat', 'broken-tempo', 'drag kick', and 'cross-over kick'?"

The answer is simple: *All* of the modern kicking tempos are based on the six-beat rhythm!

The six-beat kick has been the "classic" tempo for decades because it blends comfortably into the natural gait of the rolling stroke. It blends in for the simple reason that one-half of six is three—*an odd number*! This permits a *one*-two-three, *one*-two-three, etc., twice in each complete stroke cycle, which in turn allows each leg to blend into the lining up (streamlining) of each body-half, thus: *Line-up*, two, three; *line-up*, two, three; and so on. The odd-number factor shifts the accent nicely from one side to the other (with an eight-beat rhythm this can't happen, for example).

The two-beat, four-beat, broken-tempo, etc., kicks of today's swimming are nothing more than six-beat rhythms but with some of the beats omitted. The kicks that do occur happen precisely when they would if all six kicks were to take place. Just as in music with six beats to the bar it is possible to have *note-note*-rest/*note-note*-rest, the four-beat freestyle kick is really *kick-kick*-rest/*kick-kick*-rest. Similarly, the two-beat kick is *kick*-rest-rest/*kick*-rest-rest, with each body-half alignment coinciding with the initial beat of what would be a *one*-two-three/*one*-two-three of a standard six-beat rhythm. In the same vein, the broken-tempo kick might be: *kick-kick*-rest/*kick*-rest-rest, or *kick-kick-kick*/*kick*-rest-rest, or any other uneven arrangement. Most broken-tempo freestylers use a variety of kicking patterns—sometimes in a single race—but the first and fourth beats of the basic six-beat rhythm remain as constants. Even the so-called "cross-over kick" can be seen to operate within the six-beat framework.

Once the direct relationship of the leg actions to the total body alignment(s) is recognized for what it is, the memorizing of complicated rules of thumb for the "correct" timing of any of the kicking tempos—such as "foot 'A' down as hand 'D' enters"—can be dispensed with. The coach and his swimmers merely seek out comfortable, natural, and streamlined alignments of body-halves; the key beats of the kick are encouraged to blend naturally into these alignments as the swimmer rolls.

A *tip:* When a swimmer swims away from an observer, the natural timing just discussed should manifest itself in the form of the sole of one foot appearing at or above the surface just as the palm of the opposite hand clears the water at the beginning of its recovery swing. This relationship is especially noticeable when the swimmer is deeply tanned, the two light-skinned patches, sole of foot and palm of hand, should "flash" at the same time. If they do not then the swimmer is "out of step" with himself.

A further tip: This breakdown of the desired rhythm is sometimes caused by pushing too far back with the hands; at least I have found that in many cases a slight shortening of the pushes can bring the swimmer back into "synch"; in fact, I have found that a slight shortening of the pushes can break a swimmer loose from the confinement of a disheartening "sticking point" or "plateau" in his development (more on this later, when I discuss the arm action).

The independent leg drive, and other such outmoded kicking ratios as eight-beat and twelve-beat (they were religiously taught not so many years ago) do not divide into odd-number halves so the hips are effectively confined to a constant, level position, and rolling is inhibited—which must have pleased the "experts" of the old "thou shalt not roll" persuasion. But even the body-aligning advantages of the basic six-beat cadence can be nullified, I have seen, for example, six-beaters who were exactly out of step with themselves, and hopelessly flat in the water, so mechanically had they been taught.

I have found that the ideal timing of the kick will literally find itself if a swimmer does a lot of semi-arms-only swimming. When he "plays down" his kick and allows the legs to lazily fit into the stream, as it were, the slinky alignments of the body-halves will occur when they should, instinctively abetted by the legs. To that end, I prefer my swimmers to do most of their arms-only (pulling) training swims with the legs unfettered. I allow them to find the kicking rhythms that suit them.

Two types of kick
It's not generally recognized that the legs in freestyle can contribute to the total stroke in two distinctly different ways. They can propel the swimmer forward, and they can serve as direction-control units—rudders, if you like—that guide and tip the swimmer into the streamlined alignments of the body-halves described earlier.

The propulsive form of the flutterkick sees the legs bending at the knees somewhat more than they do for the position-control form of kick. The extra bending permits a more rearward thrusting action which at slow swimming speeds can help drive the swimmer forward.

The position-control kick is more straight-legged. The legs

merely "give a little" at the knees—as a stiff fishing rod might give—and then spring straight again with each kick.

To appreciate the difference between these two types of leg action, lie prone in the water without a kickboard and kick slowly, first with a pronounced bending and straightening of the legs at the knees, then kick from the hips with virtually no bending of the knees. In the first type of kick, the hips remain relatively level and there is some forward movement of the body. In the second type, with the legs straighter, the kicking imparts a rolling action to the torso and there is less forward progress.

The immediate and most "obvious" conclusion one might reach from this is that the kick that delivers the greater forward propulsion is clearly superior, and that is what most of the "experts" have preached, without modification, since the advent of the flutterkick. They were, and are, wrong!

The body-tipping, direction-giving aspect of the leg action has, to my knowledge, never been given the attention it deserves—its function has never been advanced in print before, even though it is the primary contribution of the legs in today's faster freestyle.

The old, often-asked question, "How much of the total propulsion in freestyle comes from the legs?" has produced many, mostly uninformed "guestimations". I will not offer another one here except to say that the comparison involved is somewhat ludicrous.

Many have observed that "full-stroke" is faster than "arms-only" and have proceeded to work out the differences in speed to "prove" that x per cent of the propulsion comes from the legs. One might as well use the same approach to "prove" that a rowing shell's extended rear length and rudder propel the craft because higher speeds are possible with them than without.

It is time we recognized that the leg action in modern, high-speed freestyle contributes virtually nothing in the form of forward propulsion, but that the legs in their role as "steersmen" are vital to the stroke. They add tapered length to the body, which is a distinct advantage in terms of fluid mechanics, and they forcefully aid the swimmer in finding and holding the most advantageous alignments of his body-halves. In this latter role they are often called upon to work very hard. It is not at all unusual, for example, for a swimmer who appears to be using a subdued, trailing type of kick to comment on how tired his legs are after a race.

Most successful coaches agree that the legs must be well-conditioned no matter what rhythm or pattern of kick the swimmer uses; it is wise to routinely include generous doses of hard kicking practice in workouts.

In order to understand the role of the kick, I suggest a study of the several stroke sequence illustrations in this book, noting that in each the same basic lining up of the body-halves occurs twice in each complete cycle. Especially observe how the legs blend into the alignments no matter what kicking tempo is used.

Rolling in freestyle

Perhaps the least-questioned of the left-over-from-yesteryear dogmatisms on freestyle is the one that might be paraphrased as "Thou shalt not roll!" Its originators, and perpetuators, could not be more wrong, and generations of swimmers have been tragically handicapped because of it.

The truth is that a swimmer in the flat, shoulders-level position at the surface is in the *worst* position available to him; he must contend with up to 50 per cent more drag as a result of frontal resistance than he encounters when tipped on his side at the surface.

The body on its side at the surface is narrower. It deflects the water it passes through in two directions, as a ship does. When squarely on its breast while at the surface it is wider and, like a barge, it deflects the water mainly in one direction: downward.

Let's take a swimmer who is, say, 10 in. thick from front to back through the chest and see what we get. As he moves through the water on his side he deflects the displaced water 5 in. to either side; in the flat position he deflects it perhaps 9 in. downwards (he does float a little and some water will escape around either side). In calculating the work required to maintain the same forward speed in the two positions we must find out how much work is involved in moving the water out of the way (displacing) while in each position. To do this we square the separate distances of water deflection. On the side we therefore come up with $5^2 + 5^2$ (or 25 plus 25) for a total of 50 units of work. In the flat position we find that 81 units are required ($9 \times 9 = 81$)—62 per cent more work required while flat! I grant that I have oversimplified things in my calculations, but this is basically the case. (Ships that are built for speed, such as warships and ocean liners, are designed to deflect water in two directions—to either side.)

As stated earlier, we are incapable of hydroplaning under our own power. We should therefore strive to shape ourselves better to penetrate *through* the water, which means that while at the surface we should avoid the flat, barge-like attitude and spend as much time as possible shaped for better water splitting.

Swimmers with *feel* going for them instinctively roll somewhat abruptly from side to side as they freestyle, spending as little time as possible in the high-resistance-producing flat, in-between position. For example: If it takes, say, 60 frames of movie film to record one complete stroke cycle (slow motion), then the chances are that 25 of the frames will catch the swimmer tipped to one side, 25 to the other side, and only 10 will catch him passing through the less-efficient middle zone.

The role of the semi-stiff-legged kick discussed earlier can now be seen to be indeed vital to economical swimming. The resistance it helps eliminate by acting, on cue, to tip the body from side to side more than makes up for any forward thrust it lacks.

Spitzian freestyle in one lesson—via The Time Machine
Years ago I recognized that freestyle, or "front crawl", in its slinkiest, most sophisticated form—as used by Mark Spitz, for example—is nothing more than "grown up" dogpaddle, and I hit on an unorthodox but highly-effective "evolve-it-yourself" method of shortcutting the teaching of the ultimate freestyle technique to individuals and whole groups. It is no idle claim that in one lesson my "Time Machine Method" can have swimmers (who can already swim) closely approximating Spitz's style. Repeated exposures to the method over a period of a few weeks can implant it as "second nature".

The beauty of the time machine method is that "it all comes about so naturally". With a minimum of words from the coach, the "ultimate" stroke develops itself—like a Polaroid colour film. The classic bent-arm pull "happens". The recovery movements of the arms become Spitzian in character. *Feel of the water* is heightened; this manifests itself in the swimmer's new understanding of the way water wants to be handled. The timing of the armstrokes, one to the other and to the natural cadence of the overall rhythm. Everything falls into place. And it all happens *naturally*. It's as simple as that. Instant Mark Spitz!

The developmental steps for teaching/learning this superior brand of freestyle via the Time Machine are as follows:

TIME MACHINE SEQUENCE

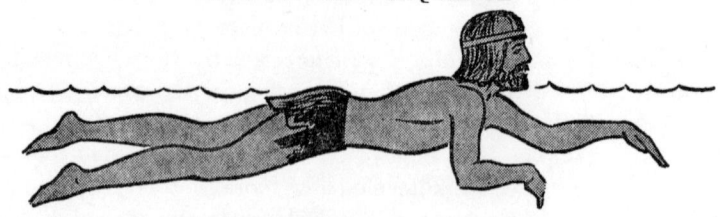

Primitive dogpaddle—10,000 years ago

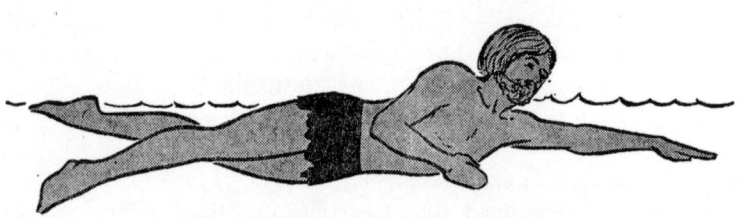

Racing dogpaddle—10,000 years ago

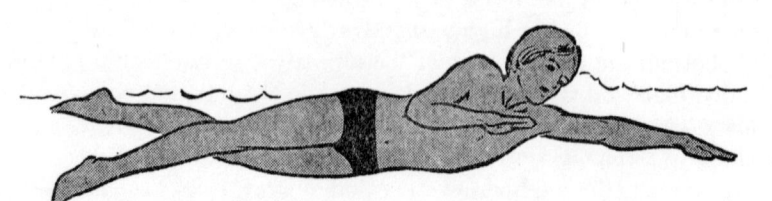

Evolutionary stroke—7,000 years ago

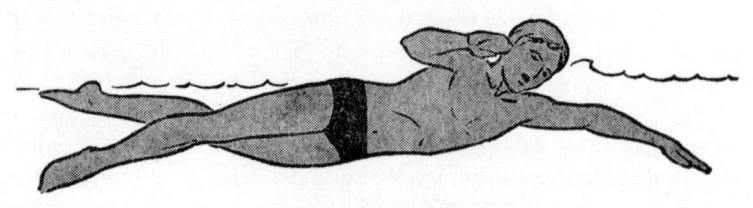

Evolutionary stroke—3,000 years ago

FREESTYLE

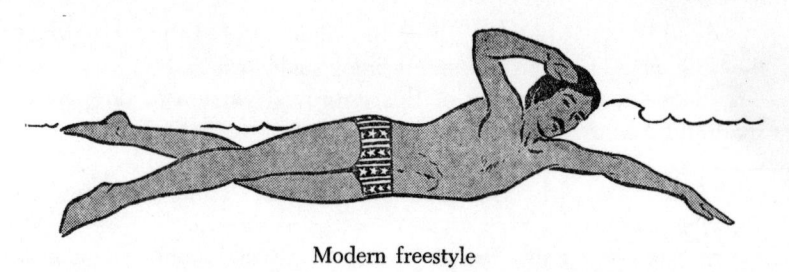

Modern freestyle

One: Have the swimmers do regular dogpaddle until it is relatively smooth and they can keep their hips and legs high in the water. The kick (flutterkick) should be somewhat subdued (most will over-kick at first). Breathing should be natural; at this point it does not matter if the face is held clear of the water. The idea is to become proficient at the "animal stroke" our distant ancestors used thousands of years ago.

Two: The chances are that there was a "Mark Spitz" way back then, *i.e.*, there was someone who could out-dogpaddle the others. He probably did it by rolling his body abruptly from side to side, the better to split through the water. He must have speared his arms farther out in front, for longer pulls, in time with his pivoting shoulders. He is certain to have let his legs wander as they kicked, sometimes in the vertical plane, sometimes diagonally toward either side. He found that by rolling he could lower his head somewhat and breathe to the side and still have his eyes and mouth clear of the surface when he needed them.

So the second step in the Time Machine Method is to have the swimmers learn the "racing dogpaddle". Have them spear their forearms farther forward, fingers pointed, as they stroke in a sidestroke position first on one side and then on the other. Instinctively, they will soon learn to bend their arms both when pulling and when thrusting them forward through the water (recovering), the better to increase the tempo of their rolling and stroking. Be critical at this stage, insist on a pronounced rolling gait, longer and longer strokes out in front, and a subdued but relatively steady kicking action with the legs well up in the water. This racing dogpaddle must be evolved beyond the embryo stage and mastered if the method is to work as it should. All traces of the stodgy, lie-flat type of dogpaddle should be eradicated.

Dogpaddle races help in selling the advantages of the racing dogpaddle. Even veteran swimmers enjoy such sprints.

For most, the learning of this improved version of dogpaddle should take only about 10 minutes, if that.

Three: We are now ready to set the "Time Machine" in motion.

At this point I like to spin a yarn to my swimmers about how the pool has magic qualities—it is in reality a time machine that can take them through the centuries and millennia as they swim along. (Even older, experienced swimmers seem to enjoy such pretending.)

I tell them that at the beginning of one-length swims they are back in time 10,000 years—it is the year 8,000 B.C.—and that they are to start off each length using their improved, rolling-spearing dogpaddle—the "freestyle" of 10,000 years ago—and then as they progress down the pool they should raise their recovering arms and hands higher, bit by bit, stroke by stroke, nearer and nearer to the surface, up to and along the surface, one finger exposed, two fingers, three, four, and so on until near the end of the length—when they are almost up to the present time—their forearms and hands are spearing *through the air* but still using the same tempo and general shapes they used when dogpaddling. In this one swim, from 10,000 years ago up to the present, dogpaddle evolves smoothly into the *feel*-charged stroke of Mark Spitz.

It's all there, the rhythm, the length of "stride", the easy ghosting-coasting along of natural, "liberated" *free*-style.

Experienced swimmers who have been brought up on the usual, heavy, uninspired "rub-a-dub" sort of freestyle are usually amazed and delighted at the sensuousness and easy-riding *feel* induced by this "stroke progression" (literally, it *is* a stroke progression). Swimming takes on a new dimension for them.

From "Chicken Wing" to "Power Stroke" in one lesson
There will always be some who will, because of their temperament or lack of coordination, or both, have difficulty grasping the subtleties of swimming, yet who love to excel in competition. The time machine method may not be for them, so I sometimes use another progression which produces a less artful but nevertheless effective style. This second progression, which I call "Chicken

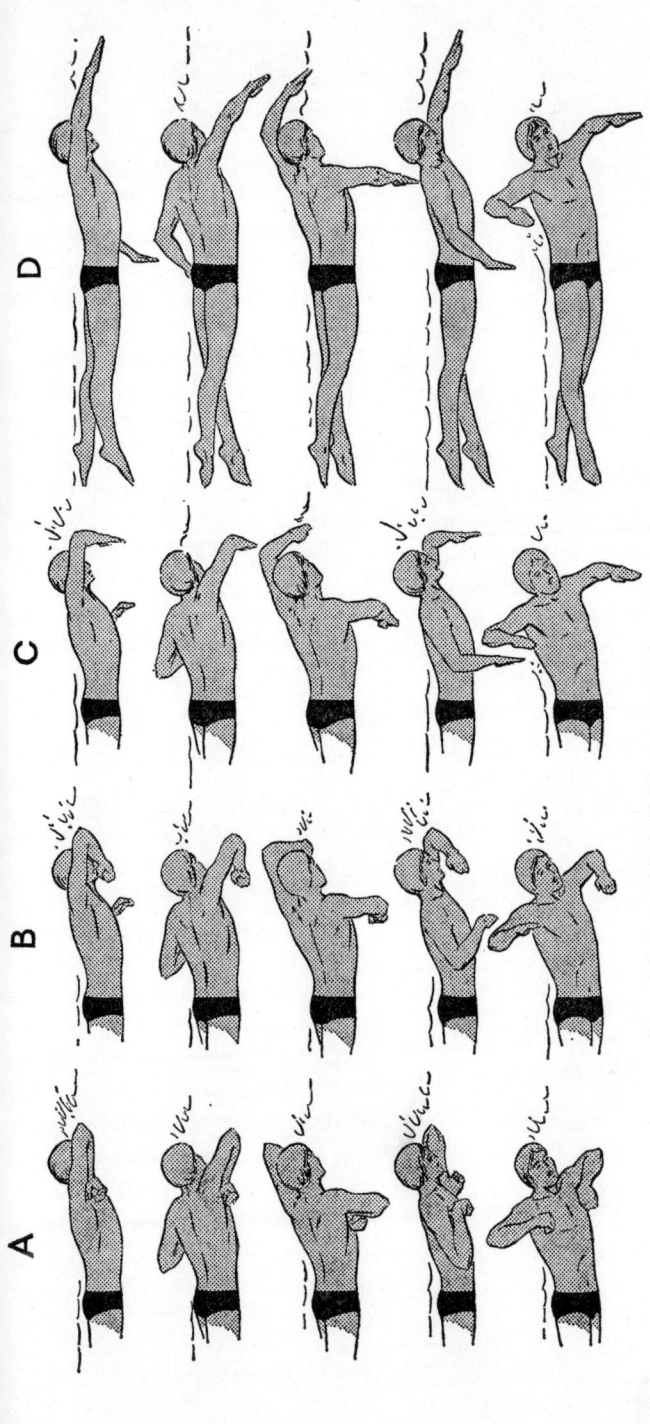

CHICKEN WING/POWER STROKE PROGRESSION

Column A shows the pure chicken-wing, with the thumbs in tight to the armpits. Column B shows the hands slightly away from the armpits as the swimmer strokes. Column C shows the stroke opening still further on the way to the ultimate stroke. Column D depicts the fully developed power-stroke as used by many top swimmers.

Wing", is based on an old but now little-known "shoulder mobility" swimming drill; in fact, the drill led inadvertently to the creation of the progression.

The basic exercise, which is known by several names, involves swimming a form of stubby-armed freestyle while holding the thumbs tight to the armpits; hence the name "chicken wing". The basic drill indeed forces the shoulder to be more mobile. Basic chicken wing looks, and is, hard to do. It is anything but a fast way to swim—in its pure form, that is.

Some years ago I was rounding off a group workout in a short course pool with a lot of one-length sprint races. As I often do, I had the squad doing various "fun" strokes near the end (leave them laughing): things like dogpaddle (while barking), inverted butterfly, "killer whale" stroke, etc., and I had them sprint "chicken wing" (while squawking). In their desperate efforts to out-chicken wing each other, I noticed some of them "cheating": They were allowing their hands to move some inches away from their armpits with the result that the stroke reminded me of the so-called "power-stroke" of Mike Wenden, the 1968 Olympic sprint champion. A light flashed on in my brain, and the chicken-wing to power-stroke progression was born. I have used it frequently ever since. It goes like this:

One: Teach the group the basic chicken-wing shoulder-mobility exercise stroke. The upper torso should be relatively high in the water, the hips slightly lower. The head should be kept tilted back on the neck and not allowed to bob. Breathing may be done to the side in time with an arm stroke. There should be enough kicking to keep the legs high. Chicken wing is not fast, and at first it is awkward for many—not many like doing it; it has none of the sensuousness of the racing dogpaddle. But it leads into good things.

Two: They start off on a length doing pure chicken wing, thumbs in tight to their armpits. Then, in a progression similar to that used in the time machine method, they gradually, stroke by stroke, allow their hands to move away from their armpits. Stroke by stroke the angle of the sharply-bent elbows is opened—as if the glue holding the original chicken wing position is softened by the water and gradually lets go. In time with the rolling of the shoulders, the hands, as they move away from the armpits, may be lifted forward more and more cleanly above the surface. By the time the swimmers reach the three-quarter mark of the one-length swim, their arms should be opened out to the preferred elbow angle of both the bent-arm pull and the bent-arm/high-elbow recovery—95–105 degrees, the angle of a boomerang (I kept a boomerang at the pool to remind the swimmers of this point). They should then be powering their way along with these fairly rigid arm-shapes—shapes strongly influenced by the chicken-wing to power-stroke progression.

A word of caution: I have found that in any group there are bound to be a few who will abandon the progression and switch back "to their own dumb thing" of a lopsided, ungainly technique once the length, or stride, of the opening strokes approximates the stride of their usual stroke. The coach should anticipate this weakness in the drill and forewarn his swimmers accordingly.

At each beginning of a new length, the swimmers revert to pure chicken wing and then repeat the gradual opening out, flower-like, as they swim. They develop the stroke, then swim the last quarter of the length power-stroking. It's amazingly simple, and it works.

If I were a summer-club coach with a horde of enthusiastic but ragged-stroking novices to shape up in a hurry for a season of only a few months, I would rely heavily on the chicken-wing progression. In no time at all, I could expect to have a healthy fleet of high-revving, even-stroking, "hot" swimmers for short races and relays. They would be knifing their hands and forearms in sharply and with precision for each new pull. They would be "power-stroking".

The two progressions compared
Stroke drills are like medical drugs. Many of them, while undoubtedly effective, have unwanted side effects.

Chicken wing is a strong "drug" specifically for getting swimmers to use their arms and shoulders more powerfully, and this it does very well. Often *too* well, in fact. In dealing with a fickle substance like water, being powerful is not necessarily the same as being effective. Far too many so-called "power-strokers" might better be called "wheel-spinners".

The problem is that power-stroking, in its simpler forms, ignores the all-important initial, subtle "catch". The hands and arms are swooped into the water without regard to the nature of water. They rend the water. There is much slippage—"wheel spinning"; these swimmers who have a mistaken idea of what pulling is all about invariably end up taking far too many strokes per length.

There is another problem: The rapid stroke rate and the snubbed-off-in-front bluntness of the main mass of the body combine to increase the amount of resistance the high-revver encounters. Power-stroking all too often becomes a matter of resorting to a frenzied use of powerful but inefficient arm pulls to cope with inordinate amounts of drag while trying to keep up with one's more-artful and slower-stroking rivals.

On the other hand some graduates of the time machine method have difficulty registering that speed is the name of the game; they can be so enamoured with the slinky sensuousness of their new-found stroke that they don't "turn over" fast enough; and there is a likelihood of not raising the elbows high enough to help the body in its rolling.

I recommend the frequent use of both drills to keep freestylers "on course", as it were, and to allow them some latitude in settling on a technique that suits them individually. A certain amount of the chicken-wing progression is good for the would-be Spitzian stylist, and, vice versa, trips through the time machine can lengthen the stroke of an offending wheel-spinning power-stroker.

Another excellent way of lengthening the stroke of inefficient high-revvers is to attack the problem directly: In a series of short, fast, timed swims of, say, 50 metres, have them count their strokes per length; then have them try to use fewer strokes per length but *swim the distance in the same time, or better, as before.* In doing this, they instinctively alter their stroke in the right way—the coach doesn't have to talk much about details. When they have stretched each stroke to the maximum that still delivers the same time, they have found their proper "stride". This approach to the problem is best done arms-only, otherwise varying degrees of kick can influence the times, and, anyway, it is the arms we are trying to educate.

I stress that individuals should be allowed to find the style that suits them, whereupon the coach should strive to make that style as efficient as possible. In the first week a new swimmer is with me, I assess him for likely style. (It is a distinct advantage to have seen and analysed so many of the world's best freestylers.) The newcomer may be a budding Wenden, a potential Dawn Fraser, a Rick DeMont, and so on. I then simply nudge him into his "groove" through the use of stroke drills—he needn't even know he is being nudged.

Wenden found success revving at the incredible rate of 65 strokes for the home length of the 100 metres he won at the 1968 Olympics—in my opinion, it was more a display of "guts" than skill. Spitz needed about 20 fewer strokes per length to win the event in 1972 in a faster time. If Wenden had tried to use the Spitzian style, it is unlikely he would have made the Australian Olympic team. Similarly, if some dolt of an unimaginative coach had negated Mark Spitz's brilliance by forcing the Wenden-type of power stroke onto him, Spitz would never have shone as a freestyler.

Stroke rate
"Stroke Rate" applies more correctly to the rapidity, or tempo, of stroking—the r.p.m.—than to the number of strokes per length. My method of "reading" stroke rates is simple; I time how long it takes a swimmer to do five complete strokes; it may be 4.7 seconds, 3.8 seconds, 5.6, or whatever. "Samples" may be taken at any point as the swimmer swims. In a short course pool, I time three complete strokes, there being less straightaway. Several "samples" may be taken in a single length to see if the swimmer is "winding down". After a while, the coach's knowledge of his swimmers' best sprint rates, distance rates, etc., can help him in the final preparations for serious competition. He may simply make stroke-rate checks instead of counting strokes per length.

I have made stroke rates into a "game" when a squad is tapering. One at a time, the swimmers swim one length as I take repeated readings and then, as each finishes, I call out his rates: "4.5, 4.7, 4.9, 5.2, for example (poor maintenance of tempo); or 4.5, 4.5, 4.6, 4.5 (steady)".

Incidently, this sort of thing, and the readings I have taken, have led me to believe that the main difference between the good long-course swimmer (who shines better long course) and the short course-only whiz (who fares better over short course than long) is the ability to maintain a given tempo in the longer, 50-metre straightaway.

Stroke-rate timed samplings are equally useful in coaching all four strokes.

Head position—breathing
There is no reason for not taking a breath once in each stroke cycle most of the time in competition—timed to coincide with the recovery of one or the other arm. Sprinters, however, sometimes affect individualized breathing patterns which they and their coaches have arrived at after trial and error. For example, they may take a breath on every third or fourth stroke during the first 25 metres, then every other stroke for the next 25 metres, then every stroke for all but the last five metres of the race when they do not breath at all in their final drive to the wall. Other sprinters might use a completely different breathing plan.

Such breathing patterns were more common in the days of the old, shoulders-level freestyle. It was presumed—it was an "of course" of the type discussed earlier in this book—that the act of turning the face to the side for the breath could destroy the perfection of the then-current "ideal" shoulders-level-flat body position. Now we know that rolling the shoulders is not a "fault" but in fact an essential feature of the total stroke. The turning of the face to one side in time with the rolling has little effect on the stroke itself. So we might as well breathe in time with the natural cadence of the tilting of the torso from side to side. In short, it costs nothing to breathe, especially if the head is slightly raised, face foremost, with the waterline coming at about the eyebrows.

A few years ago, much time was devoted to the teaching of the actual inhalation and exhalation of air. Lately, this seems to be largely ignored in the high-mileage programmes around the world. "They'll breathe in order to survive" seems to be the thinking. To some extent, I go along with that, but I have found that not infrequently the swimmer who is a poor finisher in endurance events—and even the 100 is an endurance event equivalent to the 400 in track—is limited by faulty breathing habits.

The main problem is not in the inhaling but in the blowing out. Successful Olympians invariably check out as superior to the general average in their ability to expel air rapidly and completely.

It follows, therefore, that the coach should routinely give his swimmers breathing drills—especially to those who seem to be stuck on a performance "plateau". I prefer to do this when the swimmers are working and using up oxygen, otherwise it amounts to hyperventilation which can induce dizziness; usually, I have the swimmers "on the wall" kicking as they work on their breathing, they should breathe in through the mouth and out, steadily and hard, through the *nose* and mouth. Once learned, this can make the swimmer feel cleaner and less water-bothered about the nose. He feels more aggressive, *i.e.*, more like an athlete who happens to do his competing in water.

Serious swimmers, no matter what their stroke speciality, should have their nasal passages checked by a medical specialist; we humans often have minor defects, polyps, and the like which are of no consequence until we attempt endurance activities. Many of my swimmers have benefited from minor surgery, done in the doctor's office.

Freestylers should learn to breathe with equal ease to either side, even though they may continue to favour one side. Most of the "faults" in the use of the arms show up on the swimmer's "off side"—the side opposite to his usual breathing side. He simply cannot see, or visualize, what he is doing on that other side, so he recovers "funny", drops his elbow upon entry, glides too much on that side (to delay things while he has his mouth open, breathing), and so on. The coach can spend thousands of words trying to correct these all-too-common faults, or he can, in his sageness, calmly suggest that the swimmer breathe on the other side for a while, till the problems right themselves.

To offset this kind of lopsidedness, "bilateral breathing" is advocated by many coaches, especially during training sessions. The swimmer changes breathing sides regularly and breathes in time with every *third* individual arm stroke. He breathes on the right, stroke, stroke, then left, stroke, stroke, and so on. This pattern predates my involvement with the sport and is still valid —in training. I have used it a lot but I question its worth in competition. For one thing, it tends to influence swimmers into being "one speed artists"; the style becomes more important than the speed—and that's bad. Also, it can handicap a swimmer in a hard distance race by shortening his supply of needed oxygen. This last was brought glaringly to the fore when in the rarified air of Johannesburg (altitude, 6,000 feet) one of my swimmers, Jane Hughes, a bilateral breather then, and a former world record holder at 880 yards, was in real breathing trouble. I tried to switch her back to one-sided breathing on the spot, but it was "unnatural" for her, so steeped was she in the bilateral pattern.

Now, rather than bilateral breathing, I routinely have my swimmers breathe to the same side of the pool going and coming. I ask them to pretend that they are keeping an eye on their valuables which are on a bench at one side of the pool. So they go down the pool looking to that side on each breath, and they come back still looking to the same side of the pool. I specify which side, which means that I can spot those who are "cheating". It's simple, and it works. Sets of repeats may be done this way. But in competition I merely tell them to look around from time to time to keep track of their rivals. To not be able to see the other way to see one's rivals is pretty "Mickey Mouse"—bush league!

The arms—how best to use them

I am assuming the reader has seen enough freestyle to at least have a rough idea of the arm action. But there are arm actions and arm actions: some good, others just as good, some not so good, and some that are worse still. And there are refinements not generally known even by veteran coaches.

Ideally, the body should move past the arm. The arm *should not pull through* the water, *i.e.*, there should be as little slippage as possible in the pull. I want to make this point at the outset because, for the sake of discussion, it is easier to think of the body as holding its station while the arms execute their movements—as if the swimmer is swimming against a current.

To me, the correct timing of the movements of the arms, one to the other, and to the stroke as a whole, is the first thing to get right. The Time Machine does wonders in this regard.

It's a serious error to imagine the arms as opposite spokes in a wheel, or as working like a two-bladed kayak paddle. Such an approach makes for poor pulling (wheel spinning) and poor streamlining.

The other extreme, the old "catch-up" stroke timing, in which each arm is returned to the point position in front before the other leaves that position to make its stroke, is equally poor because of the dead spots between pulls, and because the pulls themselves are inclined to be weak—even "prissy"—not to mention the tendency to overkick.

The answer lies somewhere between, but more toward the catch-up than the kayak-paddle stroke timing.

From the initial catch, which should be well out in front in line with the shoulder (*and* the hip, *and* the length of leg, *i.e.*, in line with the body-half), the hand and forearm accelerate as they sweep through the pull-push, gradually at first, then faster and faster. The average speed of the hand through the pull (up to the mid-point of the pull-push) is several times less than it is through the push phase.

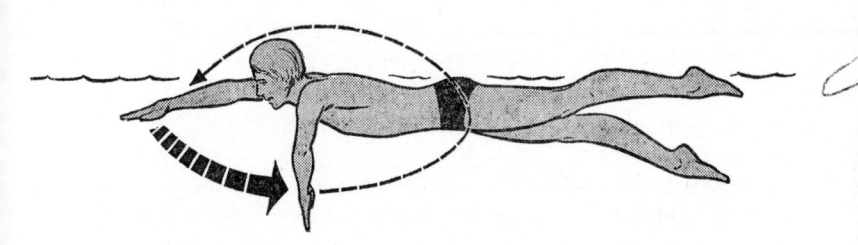

The *basic* timing I prefer requires one arm to move through the three-quarters of its complete revolution, *i.e.*, through the second half of the pull-push and through the entire recovery swing back to its next catch, in the time it takes the other arm to arc from its catch to the mid-point of the pull-push. I tell my swimmers to get the right arm back in the water, ready to be pushed, before the left arm shifts from pulling to pushing. In the basic timing, one or the other hand should always be in the "pull" quadrant of the complete revolution. I sometimes ask my swimmers to imagine that they are swimming in the dark in water littered with floating barrels, logs, and the like; to protect their face in case of collision, they should arrange to have one or the other arm acting momentarily as a feeler (as it "feels" for the catch) out in front. This basic timing makes for very smooth, steady swimming. I sometimes tell them that they have a vial of nitroglycerin—which explodes violently when jiggled—taped to their back, *so swim smoothly*!

Note that I referred to a *basic* ideal timing. I am convinced that it is wrong to think only in terms of a single ideal timing for use by an individual throughout his full range of speeds.

Years ago, I watched perhaps the finest technician ever, Dawn Fraser, warm up using one timing and then sprint to a world record using a different, but related, timing.

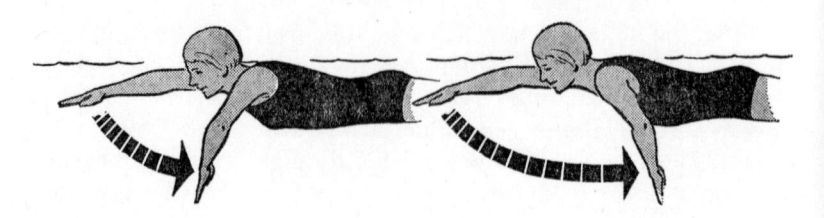

Both were natural and correct, and probably she was unaware of the change. As a matter of fact, her stroke changed subtly in several other ways as she speeded up.

Unfortunately, when a great swimmer is filmed in slow motion while swimming at top speed, only that version of his stroke is studied and copied around the world. A lie is perpetrated. Untold numbers of novices are taught to swim, slowly at first, using that precise timing—a timing the filmed swimmer doesn't use when he, himself, swims slowly.

I have long since learned to teach, at slow speeds, strokes and timings which naturally shift to the desired strokes and timings for fast swimming as the swimmer speeds up—I teach one thing to get another.

In all strokes, swimmers should become familiar with the natural changes in their strokes and timings as they move up and down through their ranges of speeds. To that end, I suggest that they cruise, and then, from time to time, as the mood strikes them, accelerate up to sprint speed for a few strokes and then settle back again—as a frustrated driver on a narrow, two-lane road might do when passing a slower vehicle.

At higher speeds in freestyle the pulling arm shifts farther into the push phase of the pull-push before the other hand enters. At slow speeds, the other arm enters in front while the pulling arm is still well within the pull zone ahead of the mid-point of the pull-push. This leads me to comment on a little-appreciated auxiliary function of the arm.

By laying an arm down in front when half of the pull-push of the other arm is yet to be done, the swimmer has extended the length of his body in the water. He now has better direction control; less effort is wasted in staying "on course". Also, frontal resistance is greatly reduced because the tapered arm splits the water with less effort than does the "bull-nose" bluntness of a shoulder (when we dive, or push off from a wall, we instinctively have our arms in front leading the way, *i.e. splitting* the way). Further, by arriving "early" for the start of a pull, the forearm and hand have more time to search out the all-important "catch"; the initial stages of the pull can then be "softer" and more controlled.

"The elbow should always be higher than the wrist." Adhering to this good "rule of thumb" is no problem except when the arm is extended out in front for the start of a new pull. At this point, some unconsciously "drop their elbow", angling the forearm slightly upward, then they exert pressure on the water which to them feels like pulling force but which is nearly a total waste of effort. When this occurs it is usually the swimmer's "off arm" (the arm opposite to the breathing side). What happens is that the swimmer rests on this arm, momentarily slowing the stroke rate so he will have more time to take in air. The coach can lecture him on this fault, citing details, or he can simply have the swimmer breathe on his other side for a while to correct the problem.

The momentary dropping of the elbows is only a problem when the swimmer attempts to apply force with the arm in that position. If he is merely lining his body-halves up so as to pierce through the water—following a gently-curved down-and-then-up route—before reshaping his arm, elbow uppermost for the pull then he is utilizing one of Rick DeMont's skills which helped him to be the first to go under four minutes for the 400 metres. DeMont accomplished this feat using an incredibly low 35 strokes per 50-metre length, so refined was his streamlining. Generally speaking, however, it is unwise to drop one's elbows, especially when sprinting.

"Olympic arms"
I have found the spinning of "let's pretend" yarns, parables, and anecdotes remarkably effective in getting points on technique across to swimmers, no matter what their ages. One of my favourite stories has to do with what I call "Olympic Arms". I tell my swimmers—who usually hang on every word during such

story times—"Let's pretend that our arms are detachable, and that we can order different ones from a catalogue of sporting equipment. There are arms designed for the various sports. There is a price-range of freestyle arms. There is the economy model at 17.50 (for casual swimmers). There are other models at 25.95 49.50, 79.95, and so on upward in price and quality, topped by the elite model: 'Olympic Arms' at 995.50! So you scrimp and save and finally your custom-made set of Olympic Arms is delivered to your home. You take them to the workout and with great ceremony you remove them from their velvet-lined carrying case and mount them in place. Your team mates are dying with envy. You have the best arms there are—OLYMPIC ARMS! You try them in the water. The difference in performance is fantastic!"

To command rapt attention when telling this and other such yarns—many of them made up on the spot to fill specific needs—I find it helps to "ham" things up a bit and act out the crucial parts. For example, I'll act out the loosening and tightening of the imaginary bolts that hold the arms on, and mount the marvellous Olympic Arms with reverent care. I seldom tell such a story in quite the same way—it helps to keep them at least partly fresh.

I then go on to explain in detail the sophisticated movements of Olympic freestyle arms. I'll use my own arms to illustrate subtle movements. On a blackboard, I may draw an arm in the key positions (complete with shoulder bolts). And I will augment the lesson by modelling an accurately-shaped, 1/3 scale arm and hand (just an arm and hand—no body) in plasticine and take it through its movements; this skilful manipulating of plasticine holds the attention of young and old alike.

The stroke begins with an arm comfortably extended in front aiming a few degrees downward. The hand and forearm search out the catch as the upper arm is rotated inward toward the cheek (the "pointy bone" of the elbow is rotated upward). A slight, initial "bite" on the water is made with the little-finger side of the hand; this helps check any tendency for the pull to stray too wide.

The action continues with the hand bending a few degrees downward at the wrist, followed by a sweeping downward of the forearm from the elbow. The elbow remains high in the water, near the surface, "pointy bone" uppermost, during the first quarter of the pull-push. This holding steady of the upper arm while the forearm sweeps down as an independent unit for the first part of the stroke is one of the refinements of "Olympic-Arm" swimming. When the forearm is almost vertical, pointing downward, the upper arm joins in and the whole arm sweeps rearward. The angle at the elbow decreases to as much as 90°, but for most swimmers it works out to from 95° to 105° as the hand sweeps under the body. It's as if the water is so shallow that the swimmer must bend his elbow to shorten his arm through the middle part of the pull-push. This shortening of the arm makes the using of the arm as a lever easier. Some swimmers of note have swept their arms well beyond the centre-line of the body, Dawn Fraser, for example. When the arm is well into the push part of the pull-push, the swimmer should consciously relax his wrist. This will allow the water to press the hand back on the wrist to the best angle for finishing the push. It is a mistake to try to push all the way back to full extension of the arm; it's much better to "let go" of the water at a point about even with the leg-line of the swim suit and lift the arm, elbow still slightly bent, into the recovery.

The pull-push will be longer at slower, cruising speeds than at sprint speeds. It is quite all right to teach beginners to use a long push through, provided they are free, within reason, to shorten their pushes naturally as they pick up speed. As stated earlier, this cutting short of the pushes can "unstick" a swimmer from a frustrating maximum-speed "plateau"; it can help him "get the lead out", as it were.

Throughout the sweep of the arms, the hands should trace a swooping, "wavery S" shape as they act mainly as sculling blades. They should scull slightly outward (relative to the rolling plane of the body), then pull backward, then scull inward under the body, then outward again; the action of pulling is essentially the same as that of an arm in butterfly doing its half of the keyhole pull, the only real difference is that in butterfly the body remains in the horizontal plane.

The relaxing of the wrist for the last part of the push helps in relaxing the forearm and hand as they are lifted out into the recovery. The end of the push and the beginning of the recovery overlap; there is no line of demarcation between the two. The body rolls to the other side—tipped over by the leg action described earlier—almost as if to roll the hip up and out of the way of the lifted hand.

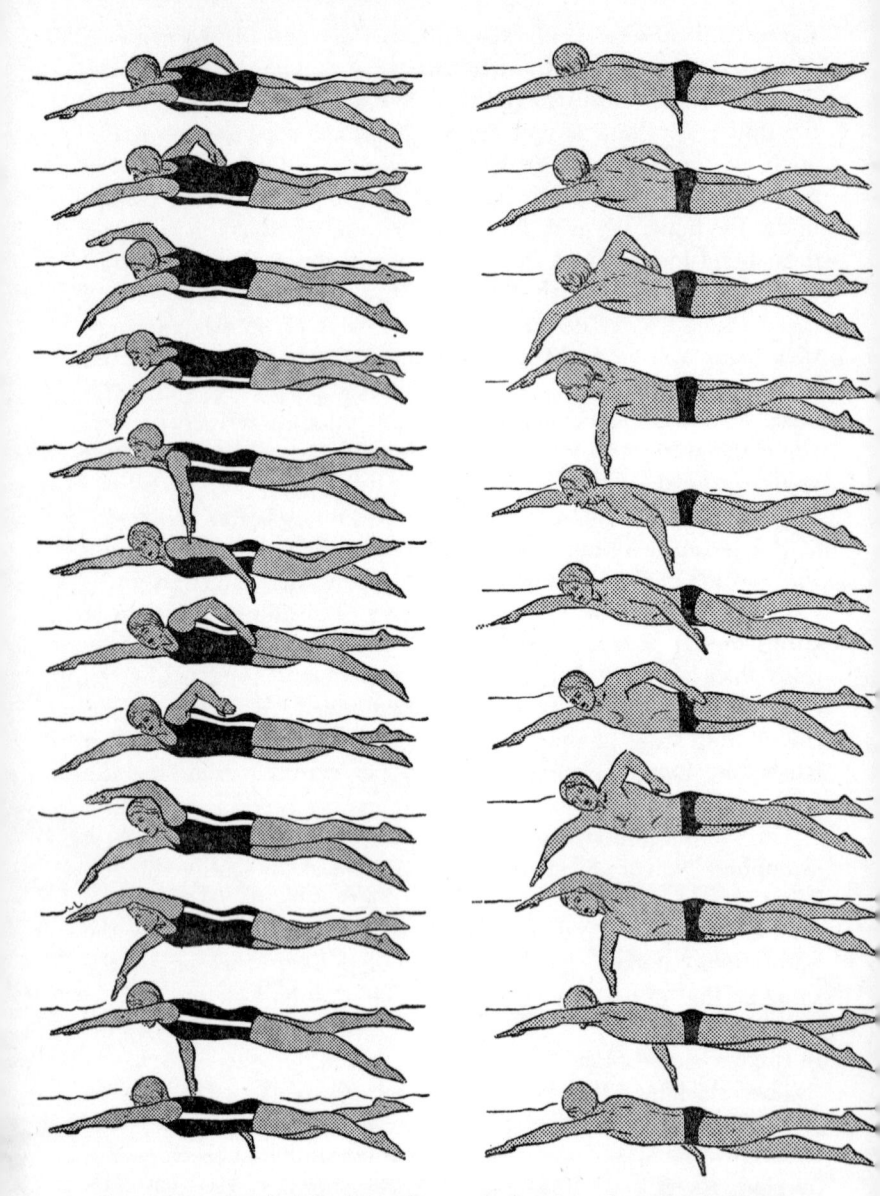

The sequence on the left shows the standard six-beat freestyle used by Dawn Fraser, Mark Spitz, and others. Note that there is always one arm fully in the water in front before the other arm shifts from pull to push. On the right is the typical power stroke, shown in this instance with a two-beat kick.

The classic high-elbow, bent-arm recovery is more than merely "stylish"; it benefits the overall stroke in several ways: (1) it makes it easier for the more-or-less relaxed and dangling forearm and hand to miss the water; (2) the weight of the arm is brought closer to the central axis of the body—its weight is less "off centre" and therefore reduced as a force opposing body rotation to the other side (a shorter lever); (3) it is less likely to adversely disturb one's body alignments—the tendency for the hips and legs to waggle is greatly reduced; (4) the re-entry of the hand and arm can be more accurate.

Incidently—and this may surprise some—the upper arm in the normal high-elbow recovery actually moves forward *under* the extended plane (imaginary) of the shoulders, well under, in fact—so far does the body tip to the other side. The action is amazingly comfortable and does *not* require unusual flexibility of the shoulders, any more than does the climbing of a ladder.

I spoke of a "more-or-less relaxed and dangling forearm and hand" a couple of paragraphs ago. I would like to qualify that and say that as the stroke rate increases the degree of relaxation is consciously diminished until at top speed, in a flat-out sprint, there should be no relaxation at all anywhere in the stroke, except, possibly in that transitional phase at the end of the push and the beginning of the recovery. One of the tricks of good sprinting is to control and shape the hand and forearm for the entry very early in the recovery—well before the hand passes the head. For great sprinting, precision of movement is essential.

I do not like the arm to reach out to full extension *above* the water and then descend through the surface. This makes for an insecure catch and almost invariably leads to there being large numbers of air bubbles streaming off the arm as it pulls. I prefer to see the hand enter *into*—*not* onto—the water about a hand-length short of normal extension and then be driven forward and ever so slightly downward as the arm extends. This piercing forward through the water wipes air off the arm and hand *before* the pull begins—the subsequent pull is "cleaner". The rolling body, which by this time is pivoting the entering shoulder downward, lines up behind the outstretched arm. The hand feels for the catch, and the cycle begins again.

CHAPTER 3

Backstroke

The ranks of top-flight backstrokers have always been thin in comparison with the other strokes. In each swimming era, the stroke has been dominated by a mere handful of superstars well out in front of the pack. Perhaps this has something to do with the nature of the stroke itself. The apprehension of swimming backwards, unable to see where one is going, coupled with the relying on groping instead of sight in executing the arm strokes, are surely factors keeping the stroke relatively unpopular. I am convinced, however, that the problem is compounded by the unimaginative methods of instruction in use throughout the world. They tend to instil an uninspired, mechanical, robot-like action rather than a joyous, free-flowing, fun-to-swim style. As a consequence, only the gifted become moderately proficient, and, of these, only a few break through into stardom.

I went along with the standard methods for years, and I had more than my share of successes—including an Olympic finalist, Eileen (Joey) Weir, in 1964. Then I had the singular good fortune to have a pure genius of a "natural" backstroker come up through the ranks of my club. Elaine Tanner, who took great chunks off both the 100- and 200-metre world records in 1967, may not know it but she led me onto the path of backstroke-coaching "know how".

Elaine amazed all who saw her as a nine-year-old. Always a tiny girl, she regularly demolished her competitors with a style most coaches of the day thought was ridden with faults; some of these coaching friends openly chastized me for not showing her the "right" way to do the stroke—it turned out that she was showing us!

The truth is that I did try to change her stroke. As a member of my club, she was given the usual, conventional drills: kicking on the back while the arms were stretched out in front with the hands clasped (ostensibly to develop the "ideal" body position); one-arm backstroke with the resting arm pointing the way forward; and so on. But Elaine disliked these and most of the other drills I was pushing at the time; she nicely resisted doing them, choosing instead the more comfortable kicking with the arms at the sides (she could always outkick her more-conventional team mates) and her own variations of the other drills.

(Elaine, who was a fine all-round swimmer, was invariably the smallest contestant in her races—she was about an even five feet tall and weighed only about 100 pounds when she won four Golds and three Silvers in the 1966 British Commonwealth Games, not to mention two Golds in the U.S. National Championships; in Canada she is still known affectionately as "Mighty Mouse".)

After a few years of marvelling at her fluid style—she took fewer strokes per length than all but her tallest rivals—and after experimenting with a wide range of unconventional stroke drills designed to reproduce her technique in others, I finally found the clue.

The breakthrough came when I realized that Elaine Tanner's "natural" method involves a mental and physical approach which is completely the reverse of that applied in the standard "manmade" or "contrived" backstroke.

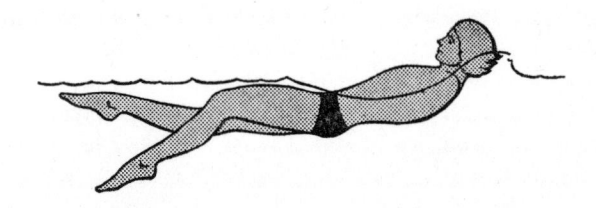

Instead of straining to lie flat and high and fully extended in the water, as the dogmas of backstroke would have it, the swimmer should be encouraged to be comfortable and to roll. The shoulders should slouch and the upper back should be rounded. The swimmer should think of the back of the neck as being the prow of a powerful ship—an arctic icebreaker, perhaps—that rams relentlessly through the surface.

I've found that pretending to be old and stooped helps

swimmers to find this position. Sometimes, as part of a "let's pretend" teaching routine, I have them walk along the side of the pool getting "older" and more stooped in the shoulders as they walk before finally falling backwards into the water and swimming, retaining this "aged" stance.

This "poor posture" set of the head, neck, and shoulders does good things for backstroke: When the shoulder joints are shifted toward the chest the muscles of the torso are better able to lend power and firmness to the arm pulls. Equally important, in my opinion, the swimmer's rounded "prow" is now able to ride him along better, deflecting the water and shaping the characteristic bow wave of world-class backstrokers (this will be discussed in Chapter 6).

It is worth noting that a high percentage of successful backstrokers have been naturally roundshouldered. This poor posture (by normal standards) gave them an advantage when it came to backstroking. Persons with good normal postures can lessen their "handicap" by assuming the slouching configuration, at least while swimming.

The following is written in the singular, but, as with most such stroke-drill methods of teaching-learning, the "system" works equally well in group situations, if not better, when demonstrators are readily available.

Elaine Tanner "natural" backstroke

Step One: Have the swimmer kick on his back with his arms relaxed and trailing at his sides. The head should be tilted up so that the lobes of the ears become little water-skis skimming along on the bow wave. His face should be clear of the water. (I'll tell my swimmers "you are in the movies and they have just spent hours making up your face—so don't get it wet".) Kicking with the arms at the side—which is perhaps the most unconventional part of the process—gives the swimmer needed practice in balancing his body around its centre of buoyancy; he will also come to realize that the thrust from the kick can be stronger and easier when the torso tilts slightly upward from the hips. (Later, at race speeds, the hips and thighs will be at or near the surface; the upper body and head will retain their higher-than-the-hips relative station and ride the bow wave somewhat higher than the normal surface of the water.) The swimmer should strive to become comfortable and "at home" on his back as he ploughs along neck first.

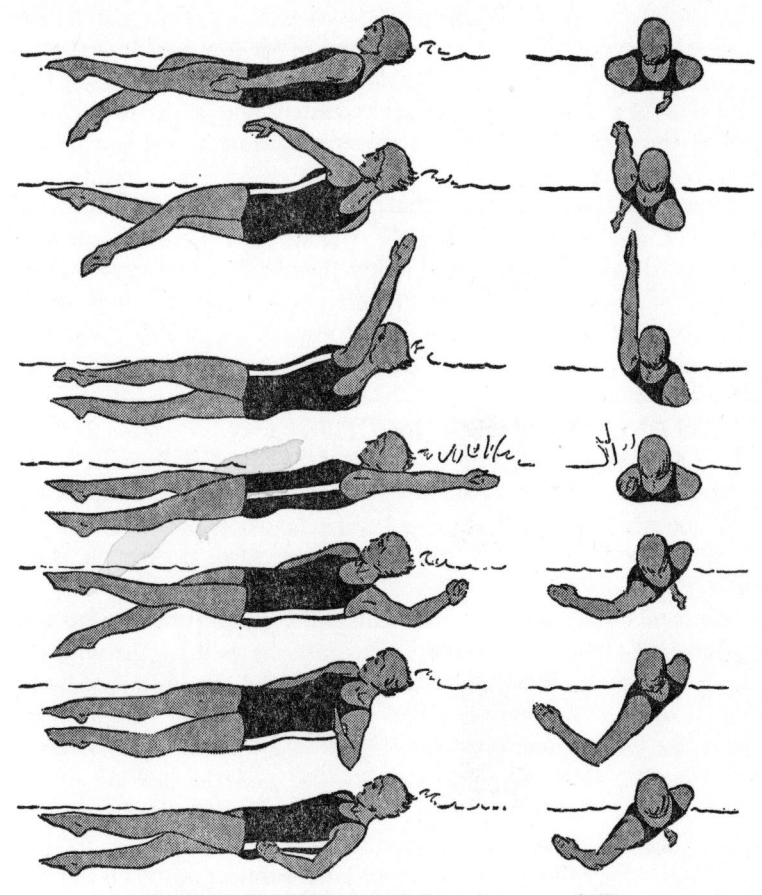

ELAINE TANNER METHODS (one-arm drill)

The flutterkick should be done with a minimum of up-and-down movement of the thighs. The knees should not break the surface although they come close enough to make swirls. It helps if the swimmer keeps his body semi-taut from the waist through to the knees. There will be two or three inches of water over his lower abdomen.

Step Two: Once the basic neck-first position is mastered,

which should take only five or ten minutes, the swimmer is ready for the next step. This is essentially more of the same only now he is allowed to "cheat" from time to time and use *one* arm to pull himself forward—"as if you are tired of kicking beside a certain person, so you 'cheat' and use an arm and haul yourself ahead a yard or so". This "cheating" is repeated over and over, always using the same arm, and with the arm pausing at the side briefly between pulls.

It's vital to the method that the swimmer raise his arm out straight and transport it directly over its own shoulder and then place it down, still straight, directly ahead of the pulling shoulder. *The arm must be straight at the elbow throughout this recovery swing!* It's easier to keep the arm straight through the recovery if the little-finger side of the hand leads throughout the entire movement.

THIS NEXT IS THE MOST IMPORTANT PART OF THE WHOLE METHOD, AND OF BACKSTROKE ITSELF: The *opposite* shoulder must roll right up *out of the water* BEFORE each arm pull is started. The head remains poised more-or-less motionless. The stroking arm is kept straight as it drops into the water ahead of its own shoulder. The other shoulder rolls up *almost touching the chin*. This causes the pulling shoulder to sink to a point almost below the head. *Now* the pull begins with the body, especially the shoulders, rolled toward the pulling side. I'll say it again: The body is rolled toward the side of the pull, and *then* the pull begins.

The rolling of the opposite shoulder and the sinking of the pulling shoulder instinctively induces the classic bent-arm pull; the coach may never have to mention it.

To get this rolling across to a swimmer (or a group) I'll tell him that he's just been promoted to sergeant and that he is proud of his new stripes and that he wants to show them off above the surface so he rolls his shoulder and upper arm up clear of the water.

I've been describing a form of one-arm backstroke. It's different from the usual in that the unused arm trails at the side. And it's different in that the other shoulder—on the "unused" side—is anything but unused; it's vital to the success of the pulls on the "good" side.

Almost as essential to the drill, and to the final stroke which will result because of the drill, is the slight pause of the hand and arm at the thighs between pulls. I know it's a lot to ask, but the reader should alter his thinking and accept the concept that the complete arm stroke in backstroke begins and ends at the thighs —not out in front. This is part of the reversal from the usual visualization of backstroke which I mentioned earlier.

Continue this drill, using the right arm over and over again, pausing at the thighs, for one length of the pool. Then use the left for the next length. And so on, until the swimmer demonstrates his mastery of this step of the drill.

Step Three: The swimmer swims as before, but now he "cheats" first with a right arm, then pauses with both arms at his sides, then he "cheats" with a left, pause, then a right, pause, and so on. The poised head position is maintained throughout. (I sometimes tell them they are electric swimmers—like old-fashioned trams—and that they must keep their noses, *i.e.*, their "trolleys", on the central power line.)

First one arm is lifted out, moved directly over the shoulder straight and dropped in ahead, the opposite shoulder rolls up, and so on, for each alternating stroke. As the swimmer becomes more and more at home in this rolling of the shoulders and stroking, he will want to shorten the duration of the hands-at-the-thighs pauses between strokes. I suggest that this natural temptation be utilized in a controlled drill which goes like this:

Step Four: Have the swimmer begin a length doing the above with rather long pauses between the alternating arm strokes, then, as he swims he should *gradually* reduce each pause until at about the three-quarter point in the length there is no pause at all, in fact he is anticipating each stroke somewhat, *i.e.* he starts lifting one arm out (with its shoulder rolled up) while the other is still in the act of pushing. In short, he begins to run the strokes together. This anticipatory action of each arm gives the appearance of regular backstroke as it might be swum in a situation when the arms must stroke through seaweed. They come out of the water as if loaded with impeding vegetation which slows the first part of the recovery only to be released about a foot into the recovery which allows the arm to spring forward. As the length nears completion, the full, smooth, alternating-arm action should be established, still showing a slight influence of the pausings that are one of the clues to this powerful and natural technique.

Strictly speaking, backstroke is a pushing stroke more than it is a pulling one. At least it helps if the swimmer experiences a sensation of relentlessly pushing himself forward, back of the neck and upper back splitting the water. The power zone of this comfortably natural backstroke begins somewhat farther into the sweep of the arms than it does in the other strokes.

The initial action of the pull helps the shoulders to roll; it presses outward, thereby helping the pulling shoulder to move down and under, nearer to the body's centre line. This action takes a little time but it is worth it. The elbow bends early in the stroke in preparation for the "catch" but the hand doesn't truly take up its purchase on the water until the forearm is warped around at right angles to the intended direction of thrust toward the rear. Because our elbows cannot bend backwards, the true beginning of the pull starts later in backstroke: when the arm is gullwinged in shape with the forearm about in line with the top of the head. This initial "get ready" action—this first flexing of the elbow—can't contribute forcefully to the pull. We humans simply are relatively weak in that range of motion. The real, forceful pulling begins about one-quarter of the way into the sweep of the arms.

Even veteran backstrokers can profit from routine reviewals of the step-by-step procedures outlined above. To that end, I have devised many enjoyable variations on the theme. For example: As a regular part of hard workouts, I'll have them swim one-arm backstroke against time in sets of repeat swims. Sometimes we'll do these using the right arm three times and then the left three times, and so on, changing arms after every third one-arm pull. "Two and two" works equally well. Then there is a progression that goes like this: 3 rights, 3 lefts, now 2 rights and 2 lefts, then 1 and 1 (regular backstroke) for the remainder of the length, and repeat, starting each length with 3 and 3. Other times I tax their powers of concentration and coordination by stipulating 3 rights, followed by 2 lefts, followed by 1 right, then 3 *lefts*, 2 rights, and 1 left, and so on—3-R, 2-L, 1-R (change), 3-L, 2-R, 1-R (change), etc.; the swimmers like this sequence, and I have found it to be among the best for developing the *feel* of the rhythm in which there are *slight* pauses of the arms at the thighs.

It's likely that once swimmers are familiar with this sort of one-arm backstroke they will use it on their own as a stroke-review exercise when warming up for an important race.

Under critical supervision, the stroke-development procedures I've outlined can bring swimmers most of the way toward world-class technique. In fact, the finished product should not be noticeably different from the technique used by such outstanding swimmers as Roland Matthes and Wendy Cook. Still, the coach may need to put some finishing touches on his creations, so some discussion of the fine points of the stroke is in order.

Head position
The head should be held neither well back nor unnecessarily high. It should be tilted up about 30 degrees from the horizontal, the better to help the neck and shoulders create, and then "ride", the bow wave (*see* Chapter 6, Wave Patterns). The head should be poised, still but not rigidly fixed; the chin should be away from the chest. The upward tilting of the head need *not* force a lowering of the hips—as is erroneously supposed by too many "instructors"; our flexible spine permits the head and hips to act independently—we don't have to lower our hips to raise our head when reading in bed, for example.

Breathing
Strangely, with all that lovely air always available, backstrokers sometimes forget to breathe during the excitement of race-speed exertion. It's therefore recommended that they settle on a fixed rhythm, such as: inhale as the right arm recovers, exhale as the left comes over. Also, backstrokers, in particular, should work at exhaling partly through the nose (but mostly through the mouth); this keeps the nasal passages clear of water, especially when face-up below the water while pushing off from a wall.

Hand entry
These days, nearly all top-rated backstrokers enter their hands directly ahead of the related shoulders. Some of the best actually "overreach", *i.e.*, drop their arms, sometimes one more than the other, inboard of the width of the shoulders, in front of the head. Depending on the timing of the stroke, this overreaching isn't a "fault" (as it was in the minds of coaches not so long ago) but

desirable. Some explanation is in order: In the old days of non-rolling, straight-armpull backstroke, swimmers were schooled to enter at "1:30 and 10:30" (with reference to the direction of the arms on entry, straight ahead being 12 o'clock). It was argued that entering higher—"overreaching"—could only result in a sideward push, pushing the flat-in-the-water body out of line. Now that we encourage a rolling of the shoulders and the bent-arm pull, the mechanics are quite different. The initial sideward-pressing phase of the arm sweep is used to accelerate the rotating of the shoulders around the body's central axis. This moves the anchor-point of the pulling arm—the "corner" of the body to which the arm is attached (the shoulder)—nearer to the centre (as seen from above) so that the body may be "towed" straighter through the water.

The shaping of the hands for the entry arouses little debate these days. The truth is that it doesn't seem to matter how the hands are shaped as they encounter the surface, as long as they are semi-relaxed; it's what they do once they are in the water that counts. Some literally smack the backs of their hands down on the water; others turn their hands palms-outward in order to slice into the water little-finger first. The grotesquely-inverted, palms-down entry affected by many straight-arm pullers of yesteryear is now seldom seen.

The backstroke pull

World-class backstrokers have been using the bent-arm pull for decades now. Its superiority over the straight-arm pull is no longer questioned. There are, however, some minor differences in the way it is used, so some comment is perhaps necessary.

When Roland Matthes enters an arm, he really enters it! His arm passes through the surface without a hint of hesitation and drives the hand forward and down to a depth of more than a foot —perhaps 18 inches. The elbow then bends sharply, drawing the hand upward to within a few inches of the surface. As the action changes from pull to push, the arm straightens and the hand is driven backward and downward. The push is finished off with a pronounced downward and inward pressing of the hand to a point some six inches deeper than the buttocks. Much of the thrust is gained from the use of the hand as a sculling blade. The down-up-down-up path of the hand scribes a large letter "W", when seen from the side, which is first cousin to the "wavery S" used in freestyle and butterfly. In fact, the track of the hand, relative to the body, and the use of the levers and muscles involved, is so similar to what happens in the other two strokes mentioned that the muscles "might not be able to tell the difference—after all, its dark in where they are". Matthes has a superb *feel of the water*, and he feels and controls it all the way through the pull-push. He doesn't drive against the same "piece" of water, however; there is very little of what might be termed a "rowing action".

Others have their hands shallower during the first part of the pull, and bend their elbows later because they roll later (too late, in my opinion). And not all top-flight sprinters use the exaggerated pressing down of the hands at the end of the push. I believe that this apparent attempt to get the last dregs of push out of each push can keep a sprinter from breaking loose into the next speed range. Those stuck on a "plateau", unable to improve their times in spite of being in better shape, should at least try shortening the rearward push of the hands to cut out of the push and into the recovery sooner—it usually works, much to the consternation of some purists who regard the long push through to the downward press as sacrosanct. There is, however, some merit in the claim that the downward press at the end of the push helps the swimmer to roll.

The amount of elbow-bend varies from swimmer to swimmer but most should strive for an angle of about 100° midway through the pull-push. This bending shortens the level-length of the arm and lets the swimmer pull with less of a mechanical disadvantage.

A common mistake is to sweep the hands too near the surface, leaving white water (bubbles) in their wake. The effectiveness of the hands as sculling blades is reduced when this occurs. The chances are that the swimmer has not rolled to that side far enough—it frequently happens more on one side than on the other. Liberal and regular doses of the one-arm backstroke drills described earlier can keep a swimmer pulling efficiently.

The arm recovery
Thought by some to be a negative, or unimportant, part of the stroke, the truth is that a disciplined, brisk-but-smooth recovery action is vital to successful backstroke.

Films show that most world-class backstrokers lift their arms from the water (the recovery starts from below the surface) thumb-side first. But when novices lead their recovery thumb-side first, they are apt to have trouble keeping their arms straight. During the second half of the recovery, when gravity comes into play, their elbows give, allowing the forearms to droop and lead the rest of the arm into a sloppy, inaccurate entry. The swimmer can't see this happening, and apparently many of them can't feel it either—many swear their arms are straight when in fact they are bent grotesquely. This "broken-arm" recovery and entry usually inhibits the desired rolling of the shoulders; it also spoils at least the first part of the pull-push. In short, it's a serious problem.

To beat the problem—to prevent it from arising—I school novices to begin the recovery with the little-finger side of the forearm leading, and to keep it leading throughout, right over and into the water. This rotates the arm so that the "pointy bone" of the elbow is on the leading side of the arm. Now, when the arm is in the downward arc towards the water—out of sight of the swimmer—the natural stoppage built into the elbow to keep it from bending backwards won't allow gravity to bend the elbow. The arm stays straight.

Later on, when the swimmer has complete command of the recovery and entry, when he has mastered the rolling of the shoulders, and when he has developed a degree of swimming speed, I make no "corrective" comments when I see him shifting, as expected, to the more-comfortable, thumb-side-first exit from the water, in the manner of the champions.

The swimmer should be urged to think of the *shoulder*, and *not* the hand, as leading the arm into the recovery; he should think of the deltoid muscles (which cap the shoulder) as springing the arm over—a subtlety of thought which works wonders. Actually, the shoulder plays a major role throughout; at the top of the recovery, the swimmer should be reaching up as high as possible, lifting his shoulder well up (it helps the shoulder clear the water, thus reducing drag and it helps the other shoulder to stay low in the water for a more powerful pull-push). I tell swimmers to reach up on each recovery as if to try to touch the backstroke turn-warning pennants. Next, as the arm is heading downward for the entry the swimmer should reach as far forward as possible with the arm *and shoulder*, without distorting the body out of line—this reaching forward with the shoulder is a little-known subtlety well worth perfecting; swimmers remark on how slinky it makes them feel. Slow-motion studies of the best swimmers reveal the recovering shoulder and upperarm almost brushing the cheek and ear, so pronounced is the rolling up and general mobility of the shoulders.

The path of the arm should be like that of a spoke of a wheel, *i.e.*, straight over the top. If it strays around to the side, even a minor amount, it tends to inhibit shoulder rolling, and thus the bent-arm pull of the other arm is affected adversely; the weight of the arm when held away from the centreline of the body (or fulcrum) exerts a leverage countering the rolling downward of the opposite shoulder.

In one of my "let's pretend" stories, I ask my swimmers to think of their longest finger as being a laser "gun" and that throughout the arm recovery they should aim its cutting ray so as to cut the ceiling (indoor pool) in a straight line directly over the length of their lane; further, I "accuse" those with unruly, or side-winding recoveries of cutting wandering patterns along the ceiling, through the windows and pillars, through the spectators . . . (stories like this help).

Body position
Backstrokers should feel high yet comfortable in the water. There should be an inch or two of water over the hips while the upper

torso is exposed to the air, *i.e.* the torso slopes upward from the hips a few degrees. From this position, everything about the stroke functions better.

The kick
There should be a minimum of pumping of the knees up and down (a common mistake). The knees should not break the surface, nor should they sink excessively. Kicking, or full-stroke swimming with a flotation device of the "pull-buoy" type pinched between the lower thighs helps get this point across nicely. The fast kicking rhythm of high-speed backstroke is best accomplished when the arc through which the feet "flutter" is somewhat curtailed. It may surprise some to learn that when the feet flop around less, when they are held in a semi-taut "ballet-point" fashion, greater forward speeds are possible. (Swim fins come in degrees of flexibility; for speed, stiffer fins are used; floppy ones are for uses requiring manoeuvrability.) Roland Matthes has used this ballet-point ankle setting for years to give himself an edge over his rivals.

A word of caution: This stiffly-pointed kicking can bring on leg cramps at first.

In training, I prefer my swimmers to do most of their kicking while holding their arms loosely at their sides because it complements the style of natural backstroke I like. But sometimes I have them hold their arms overhead in the water, elbows straight, hands clasped, as they kick. I often ask them to mix the two; up the pool with the arms at their sides, down the pool with the arms overhead. And, of course, there are numerous backstroke stroke drills that involve kicking.

During kicking-only training swims, the legs operate in the vertical plane, but during full-stroke swimming they should be encouraged to follow the lead of the naturally rolling hips. Kicking is kicking; it makes no difference to the water if the legs operate in the horizontal plane instead of the vertical, or in the diagonal part-way between. The legs, attached as they are to the bottom outside corners of the torso, can lever the body so that it rolls from side to side for better alignment just as in freestyle. (Careful study of the sequence drawings in this book will show just how similar backstroke is to freestyle in so far as the timing of the kicks is concerned.) With rare exceptions, all backstrokers use a true six-beat kicking rhythm. In backstroke we don't see many who use the two-beat, four-beat, broken tempo, etc., kicks which are so common in freestyle. The stroke needs the steadying influence of a constant kick.

Stroke timing
Since hitting on the Elaine Tanner stroke-progression described earlier, I have seldom had any need to discuss with a swimmer the timing of the arms, or of the kick—so natural is the timing it imparts. But there is a danger of over-emphasizing the leg action by kicking more than six kicks to the arm cycle. This slows the rate of the arms; it looks and feels smooth, but it is just too slow for top-flight competition. To offset this tendency, and to get swimmers generally to speed up their stroke rate for sprinting, I use a routine which has them sprinting arms-only as fast as they can swim for the first part of a pool length and then, at a predetermined point in the length (even with a ladder, or whatever), they *allow* the kick to fit into the rhythm. If they find that they have to slow down their arms when the kick comes in, they are allowing the kick to dominate the stroke, and that's bad. (This drill works well with freestylers, also.)

Why backstrokers become fatigued before other swimmers
The only way to become proficient in backstroke is to do a lot of it. Backstroke aspirants should routinely swim longer distances of, say, 1,000 metres *at moderate speed*—the kind of thing most swimmers do using freestyle when warming up or simply cruising; this allows individuals a chance to be natural, or "at home", in the stroke.

I have been convinced, however, that it is a mistake to ask backstrokers to do most of their hard swimming training on their backs. Let me explain:

Backstrokers can drive their heart rates higher than other swimmers. This is true not because the muscular effort involved is harder, but *because they swim with their faces out of water!* Yes, strange as it may seem, the simple act of immersing the nose and face in water brings about a dramatic lowering of the heart rate. In dryland tests, a subject can run on a treadmill, drive his heart rate way up, then immerse his face in a basin of water, and experience a marked drop in his heart rate. This "diving reflex"

HOWARD FIRBY ON SWIMMING

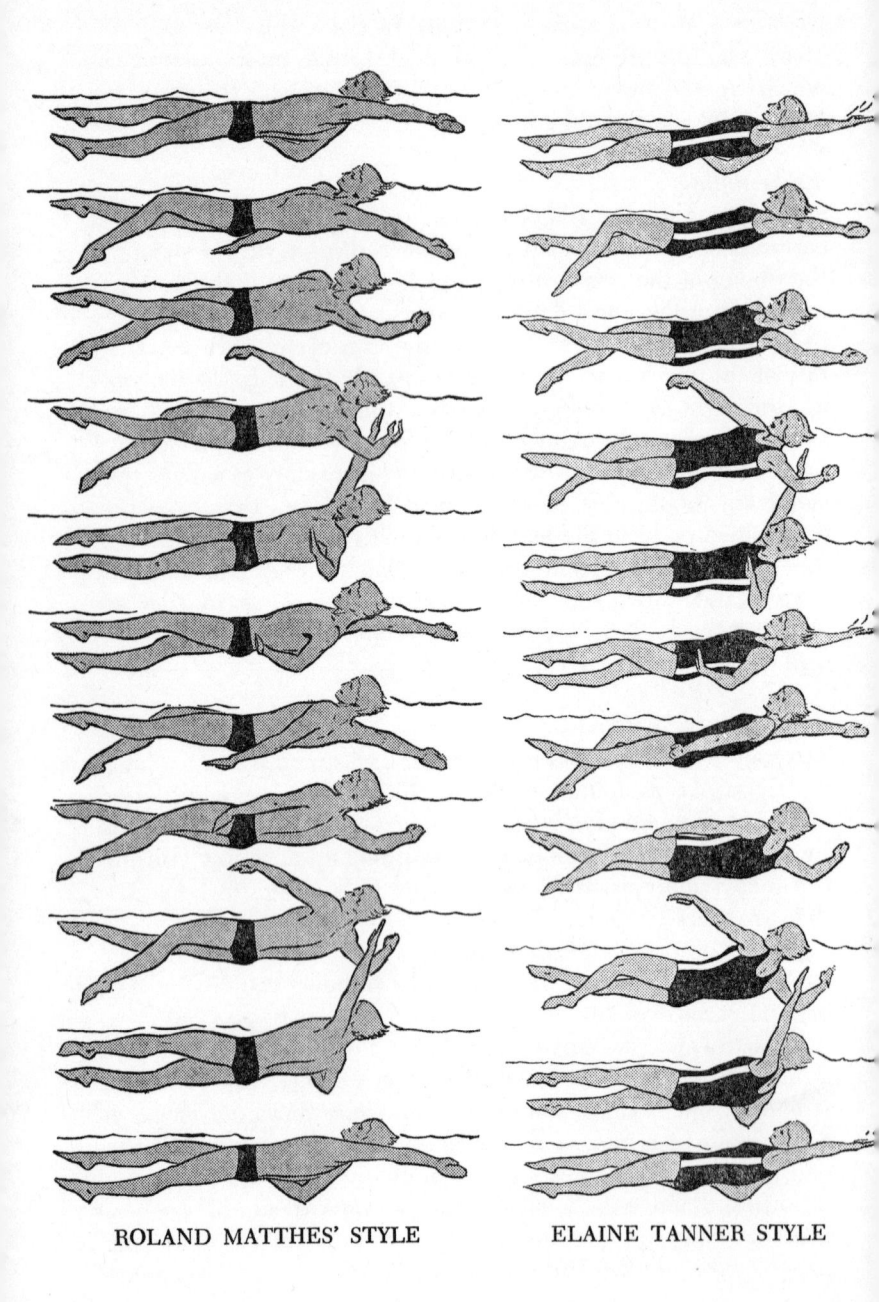

ROLAND MATTHES' STYLE

ELAINE TANNER STYLE

60

syndrome, or *bradycardial response*, directs more blood to the central nervous system, and to the heart and lungs.

It follows, it would seem, that to ask a backstroker to put in as much hard training on his stroke as other swimmers do on theirs is to ask him to experience more stress than they do. He is more prone to going into a state of failing adaptation. His chances of physically "going stale" are higher. (And I can think of a number of potentially good backstrokers who were mistakenly put on hard "swim-backstroke-only" programmes only to drop by the wayside. They weren't my swimmers, by the way!)

Fortunately, freestyle and butterfly can serve nicely as "conditioners". Most of the movements are essentially the same. So I recommend that coaches proceed with caution when training potential backstrokers, and use the other strokes about half the time, or more, for the most strenuous parts of workouts; backstroke itself should be limited to those long easy swims I mentioned, stroke drills, and to what might be termed "rehearsal swims" in which the swimmer practises specifically for the event. Such things as thirty 100s of backstroke on 15-second rest intervals are detrimental, in my opinion.

When coaching backstrokers, proceed with caution. There are few enough of them around as it is.

CHAPTER 4

Breaststroke

In the world of breaststroke *aficionados* there are countless differences of opinion on such things as how best to use the arms, the ideal width of the kick, and the timing of the breathing. So much is this the case, it remains little known that obscured by all this attention to detail there are two distinctly different schools of thought on the fundamentals of "body position".

There is the "body-flat, keep-the-hips-up" school currently the most popular throughout the world—especially in the U.S.A.; and there is the lesser-known "don't-worry-about-the-hips" school which has pockets of supporters here and there around the world—but mainly in Eastern Europe and the Soviet Union.

For purposes of discussion, and with full knowledge of the slanted implications involved, I will arbitrarily label the body-flat style "the formal style", and the don't-worry style "the natural style". (Initially I considered naming them the North American style and the Soviet style, for the two tend to divide along those lines, but such labelling would be less than accurate because there are successful exponents of each scattered around the world —"formal" swimmers in the U.S.S.R., and "natural" stylists in the U.S.A., for example.)

During most of my years in coaching it never occurred to me to doubt the absolute rightness of the body-flat pronouncements of the near-by U.S. coaching "authorities". Their preachings made sense. Their pontifications seemed so logical. That the torso should be held flat at the surface was a fixed cornerstone in my mind all the while I was becoming more and more fascinated by the challenge of coaching the stroke.

In 1964, at the Tokyo Olympics, and again at the Mexico City

Olympics in 1968, I studied, filmed and sketched nearly all of the outstanding breaststrokers. I haunted the training pools because, more than anything, I wanted to uncover clues on breaststroke technique that might help Canadian swimmers catch up to the world in the stroke. I was especially anxious to learn what it was that the Soviets were doing that allowed them to be so singularly strong in breaststroke. I had reasoned that their consistent depth and strength in this one stroke must be linked to technique because in the other strokes their record, although by no means weak, was not remarkable; surely, I thought, their knowledge of conditioning and fitness must have been applied equally to swimmers in general, yet in one category—breaststroke—they excelled.

As with many too-zealous observers, I saw, in effect, only the trees and not the forest: I became an expert on the various arm pulls and other details of the stroke while remaining effectively blind to the now-obvious truth, so thoroughly did I cherish the dogmas of body-flat breaststroke.

Then I went to Minsk, U.S.S.R., in 1969 as the coach-manager of a Canadian team. I had my movie camera with me. What I saw and recorded was a revelation. I found I was in the heartland of another, quite different and enormously successful approach to breaststroke swimming. The impact was, I imagine, not unlike that felt by a person long cut off from developments—as if by long imprisonment—marvelling at changed clothing styles and new gadgetry.

In Minsk, we were participating in a five-day, invitational senior meet; except for Canada's, all the invited national teams were from within a few hundred miles of the Soviet Union. North America seemed a long way off in another remote world— especially when it came to breaststroke swimming.

I saw dozens of very fast and obviously experienced breaststrokers swimming as if they had never heard of lying flat or keeping the hips up, yet it took world-class times to make the finals. (Soviet swimmer Nikolai Pankin, who already held the world record for the 100, set a new mark in the 200.)

It was shattering to see most of the Soviet swimmers— especially the less-buoyant men—and many of the non-Soviet challengers (Canada wisely sent no breaststrokers) swimming with a rollicking abandon as they warmed up.

I had never seen anything like it. In North America it is the artists in the other strokes who sometimes cavort during precompetition warm-ups, but *never* the staid, rigidly-proper "lie-flat" breaststrokers. Many of the male Soviet breaststrokers were unashamedly *enjoying* their swimming instead of rehearsing some stringently-formal, semi-ritualistic swimming style; they "let their hair down", so to speak, and frollicked, (in the races, all was business and legally correct).

Formal-style breaststroke
In the North American, body-flat "formal style"—a style which is taught by the majority of coaches around the world, including some in the Soviet Union—the swimmer strives to keep his body, from the shoulders to the hips, as level as possible near the surface at all times. He is often instructed to hold his "tummy" in in order to avoid introducing even a hint of "arching the back". The movements of the head, arms, and legs are all designed with a view to leaving the central raft-like body (torso) position as undisturbed as possible.

The resulting stroke, with its myriad of complexly-related details, is hard to master and difficult to "hold" from month to month. Even its most skilled users require "tuning up" frequently in regard to coordination. As with most contrived, unnatural actions, such as the military "goose step" or the riding-academy brand of formal horsemanship, the formal style of breaststroke tends to be inconstant. It is prone to turning "sour", *i.e.* its swimmers frequently find that in spite of their improved fitness and their extra effort expended, they are swimming slower. They are likely to be forever plaguing the coach for attention and reassurance as each meet approaches. (I've heard more than one well-known coach of formal-style breaststrokers grumble in exasperation to the effect that "breaststrokers are neurotic!")

Natural-style breaststroke
In "natural-style" breaststroke, there is no conscious effort on the part of the swimmer to either keep his hips high or to sink them low. (But those who want to shed themselves of the influence of a previous exposure to the formal style may have to work at arching their backs and sinking their hips at the right moments in the stroke.)

No special thought is given to the "position" of the torso. The

BREASTSTROKE

emphasis is on the most efficient (and legal) use of the arms and legs, the taking of the breath at the natural moment, and the shaping of the whole body, spearlike, for a streamlined lunge forward through the water as each full stroke cycle is completed. The hips are free to rise and fall in time with the teeter-totter-like action of the torso. There is a poise-and-lunge rhythm to the total

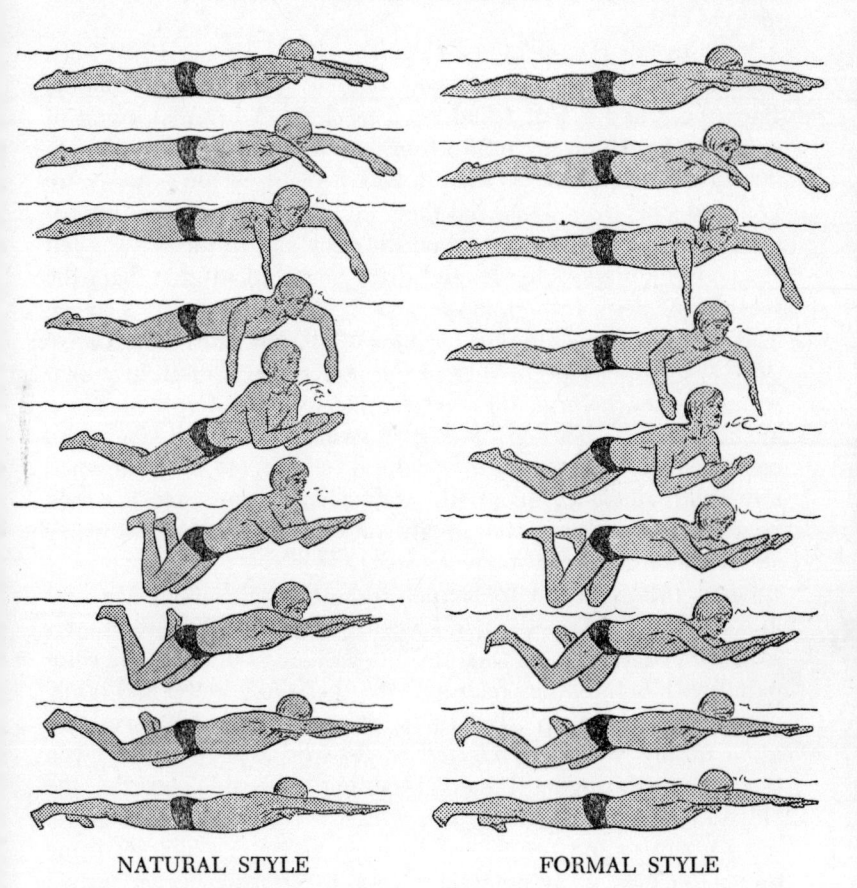

NATURAL STYLE   FORMAL STYLE

motion (some have likened this to a "snake striking"). The head moves hardly at all as an independent unit. It remains poised on the neck, tilted slightly back, and rises and falls along with the shoulders—as if the swimmer has suffered a whiplash injury and wears a light-weight supportive brace to steady the position of the head relative to the body. This lifting of the upper torso and head as a unit for a breath in time with the inward and forward sweep of the arms may indeed seem exaggerated when compared with the rigidity of the formal style. Film studies show that the poised head is teeter-tottered up and down as much as ten or twelve inches in some cases—more than the head measures from scalp to chin.

Prior to my eye-opening visit to the Soviet Union, I had been coaching a large, relatively new club in Winnipeg, Manitoba. For a year and a half I had been teaching the formal brand of breaststroke. Upon my return from Minsk I told my swimmers to literally forget most of what I had been preaching—we were going to start over! I showed them my films of the Soviet breaststrokers, gave chalktalks, and on the deck and in the water I put them through specially-devised drills designed to give them the *feel* of the "new" technique.

(This "new" technique is not new at all, but rather old. I have since seen superb engravings of the period illustrating, in underwater sequence form, the breaststroke used by Capt. Matthew Webb when he became the first to swim the English Channel a century ago. Webb swam the "natural" stroke! He was concerned more with efficiency than with "style", and, in any case, it would have been pointless in the rough water of the Channel to worry about minor degrees of body flatness.)

Good things began to happen almost immediately. My best breaststrokers dropped their times dramatically. The swimmers soon *owned* their new "natural" technique. I found that compared with before, they retained their technique better and rarely needed "touching up". But the most remarkable thing was that more of my swimmers *elected* to do breaststroke when given their choice during hard interval training; it became clear that the "liberated" form of the stroke, which invites the use of *gusto*, has a greater appeal to those who enjoy racing. (Which leads me to wonder how many potentially good breaststrokers are "turned off" by coaching advocates of the formal, lie-flat technique?)

My club in Winnipeg was based in the magnificent Pan Am Pool and at that time (1967–69) operated, in conjunction with its competitive programme, a Red Cross Water Safety (learn-to-swim) "academy" which saw some 1,400 persons, mostly youngsters, "processed" every ten weeks. After my return from the

Soviet Union (with my opened eyes) I was struck by how many novices there were who swam breaststroke with their hips low, backs arching. I'm now convinced that the "natural" style I saw in the U.S.S.R. (and which I have since seen used by many non-Soviet stars) is indeed natural. It's what swimmers will do, and in time perfect, when they are left to their own devices and never told to keep their hips up by well-meaning coaches.

The coaching *authorities* who favour the lie-flat school of breaststroke are convinced that the keeping of the torso constantly level, right at the surface—hips up, shoulders constantly so low a separate head movement is required for breathing—is the more streamlined way to swim the stroke.

Let's discuss this aspect now.

When I was in Minsk I was constantly being interviewed by students and others "doing scientific studies". ("How much weight training, and what kind, do your swimmers do? How many kilometres a day do your pupils swim?" That kind of thing—it is apparently part of the usual treatment visiting coaches endure.) After a few days of this, and after having pretty well determined what the difference was in the breaststroke I was seeing, I asked if I might interview breaststroke star Nikolai Pankin's coach, a friendly Mrs. Santa Claus sort of rolly-polly woman (many Soviet coaches are women, by the way). I had my ten-inch plasticine manikin with me and to get things started I explained, through our interpreter, how I had always taught the keeping of the hips high. I shaped my little man to illustrate this point. She smiled benignly (you poor fool) and took my little man and with her thick fingers pressed his hips down creating a straighter, but sloping alignment of his figure from the shoulders through to the knees.

And that is an important clue. Things are not always what they seem, especially in swimming. There is a less-obvious but nevertheless valid—more valid, in my opinion—way of thinking of streamlining.

If two breaststroke authorities, one of them of the "formal", lie-flat persuasion, the other of the "natural" school, were to assess the following two illustrations (taken out of stroke sequences of the two schools, each depicting the swimmer when his feet are in the common-to-both "high catch" position prior to thrusting rear-ward):

The exponent of the formal school would look at (B) and think

"Ugh, how unstreamlined, how drag producing", and it is likely he would follow up with, "See", pointing to (A), "how much more streamlined the swimmer is when his hips are up nearer the surface." The exponent of the natural school would look at his friend incredulously and blurt out, "But don't you see past the hips?; don't you see the steeply-angled thighs which couldn't be better shaped as brakes if one tried?; sure, your swimmer's torso is streamlined but so what?; the angle of his thighs rules out completely your notions of 'streamlining', don't you see?"

And the "natural" exponent could go on to point out that in both cases the depth of the knees is determined by the length of the shin bones and *not* by the location of the hips relative to the surface. Hips high or low, the frontal area presented to the water (frontal resistance) is the same, provided that the "catch" of the feet is high. The sloping body of swimmer (B) allows for a better flowing of water gradually, and without undue deflection (laminar flow) around and along his body from his shoulders to his knees. In towing the same swimmer first in the hips up position and then in the natural position, less effort is expended in the "natural" position shown in (B).

The "formal" exponent might counter by pointing out that Counsilman has shown that in a dryland situation the greater flexion of the hips (as in (A), 130° compared to 150°—the angles depicted in illustrations (A) and (B)) allows the delivery of about three times more force on the average (212 pounds as against 62 for adult males); and he might bring out Counsilman's fine book, *The Science of Swimming*, to support his case.

Now our "natural" exponent, who has done some thinking on his own and who is braced for this, comes back with an argument to the effect that dryland testing to do with swimming isn't necessarily valid. He points out that it's one thing to stand a swimmer on one leg and have him place his other foot in a sturdy, stirrup-like contrivance pressing toward the floor while holding various angles of the knees and hips; it is quite another thing to expect that against the resistance of unstable water the same readings apply. Further, he might continue, the 212 and 62 pounds (which were evidently readings obtained with only one leg and not both as would be the case in breaststroke) are both considerably higher than a tethered breaststroker can register while in the water swimming against a spring scale when using both his arms and his legs (around 45 pounds against a spring scale for a championship-class man); and a freely moving breaststroker, who has his momentum going for him, requires even less force from his legs to maintain speed. So, in either case, the available force is more than sufficient—"over-kill", as it were.

The "formal" devotee might now claim that his method is better because it leads into a more streamlined attitude of the body once the legs complete each kick. To which "natural" replies, "Not necessarily so, my swimmer, in lunging forward, can easily assume the same glide position yours can; in fact still photographs taken during the glide would not indicate the stroke style preferred by either swimmer."

In giving this hypothetical encounter I have tried to bring out the differences in the thinking of the two schools of thought. Both methods are currently successful at the world level, in fact it is not unusual to see examples of the two schools trading wins in major international meets such as the World Championships (John Hencken, U.S.A., a "formal" stylist, won the 100 in Belgrade but lost to David Wilkie of Scotland, a classic example of a "natural" stylist, in the 200; the situation was completely reversed at the U.S. NCAA (College) Championships less than a year later); it would be folly to claim either method to be the only way to swim the stroke.

To properly assess the merits of the two methods with regard to the presumed greater or lesser thrust potential of the legs and feet with either depth of the hips it is first essential to have some light shed on the truth about what makes a breaststroke kick as efficient as it can be.

The hidden secret of the breaststroke kick
Contrary to popular belief, the feet in good breaststroke do *not* drive the swimmer forward as a direct result of any paddle-like pressing of the soles of the feet backward against the water.

Benjamin Franklin, by all accounts a good breaststroke swimmer and certainly one with a lot of curiosity, surmised as much some 200 years ago. He fashioned foot paddles, similar to the hand paddles in common use today as training aids, from the flat, round tops of small kegs and found them worse than useless for breaststroke; he got more thrust without them.

And today, if we would but think about it, the swim fins used by skin divers, offering as they do all those extra square inches of sole area, are useless to a swimmer who attempts the breaststroke kick while wearing them (our breaststroke kick is not at all like a "frog kick").

The feet in good breaststroke are mainly effective as propelling surfaces because they function in the manner of rotating propeller blades. Any straight-back oar-like pushing they do is insignificant in comparison.

Without realizing it, the better breaststrokers have all along been taking advantage of the fact that a good part of the human foot forward of the ankle is shaped and contoured remarkably like an efficient propeller blade.

The thrust obtained by a propeller blade results from a phenomenon of fluid mechanics known as "Bernoulli's Principle" which states that when a fluid passes over a surface the pressure of the fluid upon the surface is reduced proportionally to the speed of the fluid's travel relative to the surface. The faster the fluid travels, the greater the reduction in pressure.

The propeller blade and the airplane wing are designed to make use of this principle. Their cross-sectional shape (foil) and their angle to their direction of motion (pitch) are such that the fluid forced over the front or top moves farther (and therefore faster) than the fluid passing behind or below. If the foil shape and pitch are right, considerable differences in pressure are created and the blade or wing is thrust or lifted forcefully toward the zone of low resistance. Giant airplanes are lifted into the air by the application of Bernoulli's Principle, and ships use propellers rather than paddle-wheels to get the maximum from their available engine power, it having been long since determined that propellers are more efficient than paddle-wheels in delivering thrust.

(In 1845, the British Admiralty conducted a test to determine the comparative efficiency of its first propeller-driven ship. The ship was pitted against a paddle-wheeler in a "tug of war". The two ships were of similar tonnage and hull design and their engines were rated the same in horsepower. The propeller-driven ship won easily.)

So here we are with feet poorly shaped for paddling—try using one bare foot to paddle a canoe sometime to appreciate this—but which are well suited to obtaining great amounts of thrust when moved so as to cause the water to flow rapidly over the instep crossways toward the little-toe side of the foot.

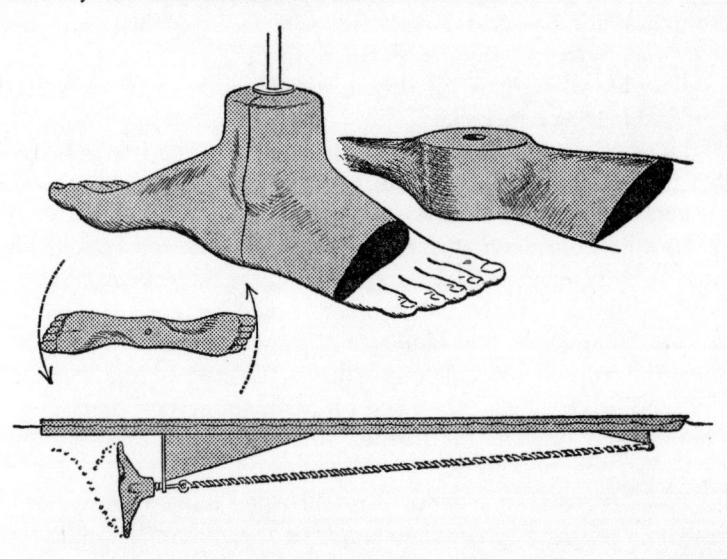

Now, a propeller blade rotates on a shaft with one or more identical counterbalancing blades. Our feet, strictly speaking, are not attached to rotating shafts—they can be rotated through an arc of only about one quarter of a circle; and that is what the successful breaststroke kick is all about. To prove this to my own satisfaction, I fashioned a propeller out of two identical feet fused to a single ankle. The feet were modelled accurately in regard to proportion and contour (as can be attested to by Buck Dawson, Executive Director of the International Swimming Hall of Fame). This unique foot-bladed propeller was rigged to a simple boat shape and was driven by a wound model-airplane flight rubber.

It worked on its first trial. The thrust generated by the rotating foot-blades was more than even I had supposed it would be; and subsequent tests, using varying speeds of rotation, revealed some significant aspects about foot-blading. The propeller was at its most efficient when it turned at a moderate rate, *i.e.* at a rate which could be followed easily by the eye; apparently at high r.p.m.s the relatively thick foil is so good at reducing pressure over the instep the water there literally turns to steam (a phenomenon known as cavitation) effectively spoiling the thrust-producing capabilities of the foil shape (one of the first experimenters with propeller-driven ships, circa 1800, had this problem until he used reduction gears to bring his propellers down to a rate compatible with the water).

All right, what does all this mean? Should we coaches start over and teach a new kick?

The answer to the second question is "no". The better breaststrokers and their coaches are already making good use of the phenomenon although they are probably not aware of it.

The answer to the first question is: Armed with this knowledge, we can be surer in our teaching of the kick; the coach's "batting average" should improve for he now knows the reason for having the feet shaped as foot-blades, *i.e.* drawn up toward the shin (dorsi-flexed) and rotated outward, for the start of the so-called kick, and he recognizes the need for maintaining that dorsi-flexed angle of the ankles as the feet are rotated through their quarter-circle arc, whipped around by the aptly-named "whip kick".

Good breaststroke coaches have all along known the value of dryland exercises designed to improve the swimmers' ability to hold and use a better "set" of the foot-blades on their shafts (ankles). They should continue with such exercises, perhaps with even greater purpose in the light of the foregoing.

Also, the coach should *consider* teaching a wider, more out-and-around sweep of the foot-blades during the erroneously-labelled pushing phase, the better to gain longer arcs of the feet through the water, the better to achieve extended and controlled thrust from the foot-blading action. Punching the feet backward and down-and-around too swiftly, as many ultra-narrow knickers sometimes do, can induce that thrust-spoiling cavitation phenomenon referred to earlier.

Feet vary considerably in their shapes—as witness the myriad sizes and widths shoe shops must stock—so it follows that some individuals are endowed from birth with superior breaststroke foot-blades. Flat sprawling feet, with their thinner more-winglike foil shapes are naturally better than narrow feet with high, thick arches. Fortunately, most are between these two extremes. It is definitely helpful, and this *is* something an individual can improve on, to be able to rotate one's feet and lower legs outward more than is usual, the better to increase the degrees through which the foot-blades can arc—have you ever noticed that many "born breaststrokers" normally walk and stand with their feet turned well out *à la* Charlie Chaplin?

I've noticed that when some swimmers with super-talented breaststroke feet swim backstroke they are prone to flicking their boot-blades around breaststroke-style, one foot and then the other alternately, so much thrust do they get that they prefer this weird form of backstroke kick to the conventional flutter kick. You only have to see and evaluate this once to be convinced of the propeller blade-like role of the feet in breaststroke.

As many a powerfully-built would-be breaststroker has found to his consternation, control and precision of movement—finesse—are more important than sheer mechanical strength. Water, being the fickle substance it is, must be caressed and not manhandled, so to speak. And because our legs are so much stronger than the arms, and because they are normally less adept at subtle movements, this applies especially in the case of the breaststroke kick. In the "force" department, power is more important than strength—and the two are different things.* Nevertheless, well-conditioned legs are a factor. Although much less force is required per kick than some suppose, the ability to repeat the required force as needed throughout a race, *i.e.* endurance, is paramount.

The breaststroke arm action

Prior to the beginning of each arm action the arms should be straight, or so nearly so that they look straight, with the hands side by side and with the elbows—the "points" of the "elbow

---

* To physiologists, power is the muscular ability to produce an effect; a common test, for example, is to have a person pull on a cord which is wound around the axle of a fixed but free-to-turn flywheel in the manner of a string around a top. The resulting number of revolutions of the wheel is recorded as a measure of the power imparted by the pull. It is not uncommon for a person with greater strength, *i.e.*, one who is capable of exerting more static force, to score lower than a weaker person. The so-called "natural athletes" tend to score well in the power to strength ratio.

bones"—rotated upward. This aids in rotating the deltoid muscles which cap the shoulders inward and upward toward the cheeks. The whole arm, but especially the forearms and hands, should be aimed slightly downhill, the hands at a depth of about six to eight inches. The hands, which should be lower than the elbows, should be tilted, thumbsides lower, at an angle of about 45°. (A common fault is the tilting of the hands slightly upward, like the tips of skis, finger-tips at or near the surface; in jest, I sometimes remark to my erring swimmers that they look like they are drying their nail polish.)

From this "point" position, the pull begins with the separation of the hands. The wrists flex downward, shaping the hands as blades for sculling outward. The elbows rotate upward even more as they bend, permitting the hands and forearms to curl around more water. This outward sculling continues while the upperarms remain close to the surface until the arms are well apart in a letter "Y" configuration. The shoulders are kept low and the swimmer's face remains mostly submerged during the action thus far. So low are the shoulders kept up to this point that water gushes over the shoulder blades, and the head, staying legal, reminds me of the conning tower of a submarine with its decks still submerged. This allowing of the water to flow over the shoulders achieves the reduction in drag described earlier in my freestyle chapter. It's legal and it is the next best thing to being totally submerged, which is illegal (because of the advantage it would give a swimmer).

There is a limit to how far outward the hands can scull effectively so at the widest point in the arm action—about three-fifths of an individual's maximum arm span—the forearms are directed rearward and "around the bend" as the "pitch" of the sculling blades (the hands) is reversed for sculling inward. This change occurs about in line with the level of the cheekbones; the upper arms have remained near the surface but now they are swept downward slightly as the shoulders rise above the surface transporting the head high enough for the breath while adding impetus to the vigorous inward and forward sculling action of the hands.

This is the most natural point in the whole sequence of the stroke (legs and arms) for the swimmer to raise his front end for a breath. As far as the arm action is concerned, it couldn't work out better. The strain of pulling is diminishing; muscles of the "rib cage" are relaxing, the better to allow the free movement of the bellows action of inhaling; the extra buoyancy of the filling chest aids in inducing the rocking-horse action of the "natural" stroke—it couldn't work out better.

It's not generally known that the inward and forward sweep of the breaststroke arm pull can be propulsive. As in sailing it is possible to tack against the wind if the sails are properly set, so can the "blades" of the hands scull a swimmer forward while sweeping inward and forward.

The hands in breaststroke must never be thought of as hoe-like instruments which "chin" the swimmer forward in a series of yanking motions. Sculling is the secret; sculling of the type used in synchronized swimming, and in "treading water". To that end, I recommend that *all* swimmers be given generous doses of sculling in their training. The fact is that a large part of the propulsion produced in an Olympic pool is of a sculling nature.

The fastest freestyle swimming speed ever attained by man over 50 yards is 4.89 mph, according to the 1974 *Guinness Book of Records*, yet lowly penguins, according to the same source, can swim (scull) at speeds of 22.3 mph. Man has a lot to learn in the sculling department.

The outward, then partly rear-ward, and then inward and forward tracing of the blade-like hands scribes a pattern which, relative to the body, resembles an inverted valentine heart. However, film studies, notably by Counsilman, show that there is virtually *no* rearward movement of the hands. The body, which has momentum, remember, is drawn forward while the hands blade outward and then reverse their pitch and blade inward. The action should be continuous throughout the movement thus far and then accelerated as the hands are thrust forward vigorously during the final stages of the stretch into the streamlined position. The final jabbing forward of the pointed hands, just described, does good things for the total stroke. It induces the desired cleaning up of the body for its streamlined slide forward through the water, submerged except for the crown of the head; if the timing is right, it also induces the final whipping together of the foot-blades. (When I have my swimmers do arms-only in training, I encourage them to rehearse this jabbing action.)

The details of the arm action vary. Some pull wider, some narrower, and a few pull farther back and around past the line of the shoulders. Some turn their hands palms up, side by side, little fingers touching or one hand actually over the other, at the end of the inward sweep and rotate them palms down and then palms facing out as they separate for the beginning of the next pull; this whole sequence is done smoothly with a continuous action—no "dead" spots in the entire sequence from pull to the beginning of the next pull—and it definitely encourages the elbows to roll upward for the start of each new pull; also, with the back of the hands downward the swimmer is not tempted to use his hands as planes to support himself, he operates naturally around his centre of buoyancy. An extreme version of the action just described, and I have seen a few world-class swimmers using it, has the swimmer actually crossing his wrists as the arms are driven forward; in trying it on myself I found that it seems to give more time for searching out the *feel* of the "catch"; strictly speaking, however, this conspicuous operating of the arms in different horizontal planes is contrary to the rules.

Rule 65, Breast Stroke Swimming, of the current (1972–76) Hand Book of the International Swimming Federation (FINA) states in paragraphs (b) and (c) the following:
(b) All movements of the legs and arms shall be simultaneous and in the same horizontal plane without alternating movements.
(c) Hands shall be pushed forward together from the breast, and shall be brought back on or under the surface of the water.

The above are "cold" facts. Fortunately, stroke judging at the international level—especially in breaststroke—is tempered with common sense. To that end, the Canadian (CASA) Hand Book—which I wrote, by the way—carries a note which reads as follows:

"In actual practice, it is doubtful if any breaststroke swimmer has ever been absolutely legal insofar as the [strict interpretation of the rules] is concerned. In the final analysis, the duty of a Stroke Judge and Turn Judge is to see that no swimmer gains an unfair advantage through the use of irregular movements or body alignments."

The arm action should be comfortable and natural and totally free of affectations. Arms-only practice and full-stroke practice is the answer and lots of it, at varying degrees of intensity. Arms-only breaststroke is good for all swimmers, even though some may never swim breaststroke in competition. It is a wonderful forearm conditioner; it is better than any other single drill at bringing on the familiar "arms turning to rubber" "caving in" of the controlling muscles of the forearms and hands experienced by half-trained swimmers in real competitive situations. If training amounts to "getting tired on purpose", the better to prompt the body to adjust and adapt, then arms-only breaststroke is great for promoting the adaptation of the forearms.

I encourage my swimmers to use a *slight* dolphin kick when doing arms-only breaststroke. It fosters the rhythm of the "natural" style, for one thing, but mostly I want them to instinctively *feel* the moment when a nudge from the rear is most beneficial—which is the moment, in full-stroke breaststroke, when the kick should come in.

Breathing

With rare exceptions, all modern breaststrokes breath on every stroke. There is no reason for them not to. It is the timing of the breath in regard to the arm stroke that occupies the thoughts of serious coaches.

The old "classic" stroke of some two decades ago called for the swimmer to lift his head and inhale while the arms were still well out in front spearing along. The head was then lowered and the arms and legs did their things. The whole arrangement made for a super-consciousness of lying flat. Some took the lie-flat concept a notch further and taught their swimmers to breathe on every other stroke.

We now know that it is better to pull first and breathe later, as it were, when the arms are, say, two-thirds of the way through their trip from point position to point position. The shoulders and head are raised for the breath, in some cases dramatically, as the arms sweep inward and forward; it is all so natural—as Capt. Webb knew all those years ago—it is a wonder it took us so long to see the light.

For many, when the action is right, there is a pronounced spewing forward of water from beneath the swimmer's chin; sometimes called "the fountain" it is used by many coaches and swimmers to gauge the effectiveness of the overall technique, especially when warming up for a race.

The combination of bow wave and fountain bothers the odd swimmer, so to keep water away from his nose and mouth while inhaling he will turn his head to one side. This is legal but in time it can induce the sinking of the "off" shoulder, and sometimes the hip as well. So much influence can the position of the head exert that the knowledgeable coach can use it in his "stroke correcting". For example: A swimmer who carries his head in the centre but swims with one hip lower than the other—which makes for a kick with one leg dangerously low, tempting disqualification—can be eased back, hips level, by having the swimmer turn his head to the side of the low hip.

Finally, on breathing, a tip for the swimmer who raises and lowers his head as an independent unit: Hold off the lowering of the head until *after* the feet have engaged the water at the start of the so-called "push" phase of the kick. The difference in the solid feeling of the "shove from the rear" thus influenced is profound—and you have to see it or use it to appreciate it. It is a common but little-known fault to lower the head, often abruptly as if driving a spike with the forehead, prematurely, *i.e.* before the feet have *left* their "catch" position. Not surprisingly, I have found that often, when the lowering of the head is delayed as I have suggested, the swimmer feels no desire to lower his head at all as an independent unit. This, by the way, was one of the last things I adjusted on Sylvia Dockerill's stroke before she won the 100 in the 1971 Pan Am Games.

Balanced breaststroke emphasis
In well-balanced, modern breaststroke of either style, "formal" or "natural", the legs *and* the arms should be used to their fullest potential, with neither department dominant. In my opinion, the natural style brings this off better than the formal style, the latter being composed of parts which are prone to functioning independently. Generally, girls tend to swim a legs-dominating stroke and therefore should be exposed to extra doses of arm-developing butterfly, freestyle, etc. These days, it is not at all unusual for a top female breaststroker to be a threat in the other strokes as well, and especially in the individual medley.

On breaststroke training
Like an exotic plant, only distantly related to the other strokes, breaststroke thrives best when given a specialized environment—which, unfortunately, it seldom receives. Skill, subtlety of move-

ments, precise timing, and specialized conditioning are of the utmost importance, yet all are hard to perfect within the framework of typical big-squad, multi-stroke, razzle-dazzle workouts. In such training situations breaststrokers are short-changed. Certainly it is wrong to constantly swim them in crowded "circles" amongst others using other strokes on long sets of short, hard, "interval" repeats where they are forever dodging their swifter team mates while trying to "hold their stroke" in churned-up water. Instead, I prefer to designate certain lanes exclusively for breaststroke swimming.

So specialized is world-class breaststroke, many nations subdivide their national teams and have separate breaststroke squads and coaches.

Darts and breaststroke training compared
Let me use an analogy or two involving the game of darts to illustrate the extremes in the approaches taken in the coaching of breaststrokers through a long season. I have no idea of how dart players train—or even if they "train" at all as we know it—but let's say I have been dragooned into training would-be dart players for the big meet ten months hence.

Now, I have the option of doing what many swimming coaches do; I can have my dart shooters do a lot of over-distance work, *i.e.* I could have them stand three or four times the regulation distance from the board and loft thousands of shots (which would surely be mostly misses), and from such distances I could have them use overweight darts (overload). Then, as the season progresses, I could have them come gradually closer. A few weeks from the championships I might allow them some chances to rehearse with standard darts over the regulation distance in the hope that they might sharpen their aim. My dart players' throwing arms, although perhaps erratic, would be well-conditioned physically! As a coach, I might even fool myself into thinking I had done an adequate job.

On the other hand, if I were to borrow the formula of some of the most successful breaststroke coaches and approach the problem from the other end of the continuum, I could have my pupils begin the season by standing only a yard from the target and practising with regulation darts until their aim becomes nearly perfect. Then, and only then, they would be allowed to work from four feet away, then five, and so on, increasing the range as they master each interim distance (and shortening the range if their accuracy deteriorates). All the while this process of skill-development goes on, I could see to the physical conditioning of their throwing arms by having them work hard on other, but related, activities such as ball throwing or chopping wood.

I rather think the second approach would produce better results in the big meet. Applied to breaststroke such a plan of attack would work out something like this:

(1) In the initial stages of the season the coach would work on the honing of the as-yet out-of-shape swimmer's technique to the point where the swimmer can deliver a time for a short distance —say a fifty—which is as fast, or faster, than the planned ultimate split-time for that first portion of the race distance (it does not require much conditioned endurance to negotiate a "hot" fifty).

(2) While the precision in (1), above, is being developed, the swimmer is subjected to real, but controlled, workloads of hard training but in the shape of things other than full-stroke breaststroke.

(3) The process continues with ever increasing workloads of butterfly, freestyle, breaststroke kicking, arms-only breaststroke, dryland pulley work—almost *anything but* sets of slower-than-race-speed full-stroke breaststroke.

(4) Periodically, say once a week, the swimmer is timed over a short breaststroke all-out "effort" swim; if in this "check swim" his technique is incapable of its former sheer speed, then it's "back to the drawing boards"; the situation is assessed and remedial action is taken.

(5) This continues until the final stretch of the season, starting perhaps five weeks before the big meet, at which time more and more well-rested "dress rehearsals" of the breaststroke events, whole or in part, are included in most workouts.

The experienced coach-reader will realize that in actual practice a plan somewhere between the two extremes is probably best; there is more than one meet a year and swimmers are not machines; they need exposure to competitive situations (meets) as part of their build-up.

Breaststroke "exercise strokes"
It's significant that many of the fastest and most durable breast-

stroke swimmers have come out of programmes in which a wide variety of stroke drills are used. There are many such drills and some are better than others, depending on the precise style of breaststroke each coach prefers. Some of the better ones are as follows:

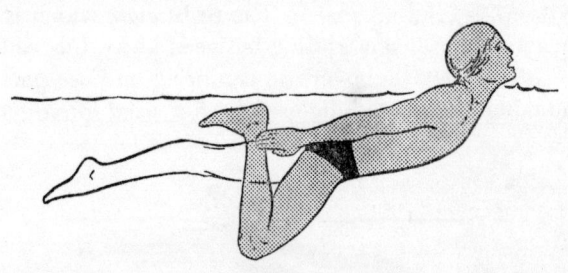

Ankle-touch kicking: With the arms held as shown, the swimmer on each kick draws his feet up high enough and far enough to touch the extended fingers with his ankles or heels. This promotes the desired open angle at the hips (if the knees are drawn too far forward under the swimmer, the touch is not possible) and it is a useful check on the symmetry of the kick. Out of sheer routine mileages covered, even the best breaststrokers from time to time are prone to becoming lax in drawing their heels up near enough to the buttocks; the result is half-size kicks, and the swimmers are at a loss to know why their times are "off". The regular use of this drill, especially when warming up for competition, can forestall the problem. I prefer the head to remain constantly up; it promotes a better "set" of the body for each kick and at the same time serves to strengthen the muscles of the upper back and neck. Swimmers find the head-up part hard at first.

Multiple-kickboard kicking: Bind several kickboards together with a band cut from an inner tube. Kicking this large, more-buoyant unit forces a steeper angle of the body which in turn cultivates the desired higher catch of the feet prior to each kick. It is much harder than kicking with a single board.

Ringbuoy kicking: Like the above but with a large life-saving ringbuoy used instead of boards. The resistance, which is phenomenal, effectively kills any gliding between kicks. Use caution, as the strain is considerable; over-use can bring on knee pains. Such drag-producing devices can be useful *when used intelligently*.

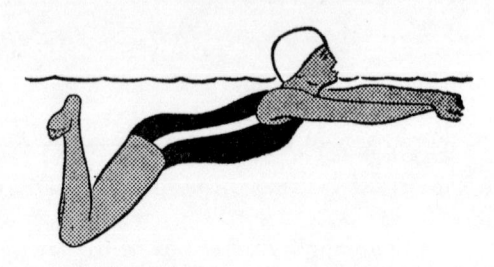

Crossed-wrists spearing: The arms are held straight, the wrists crossed and hands clasped as shown; the swimmer should stretch this "spear" as far forward as he can. This drill deprives the swimmer of the luxury of the support of the hands and fosters a more natural balancing of the body around its centre of buoyancy. It also develops a sturdier framework of the torso from which to kick—the hips sit lower and are better able to receive the driving force of the legs. It's harder than it looks. It's one of my favourites because it does such good things to the overall stroke. The head should remain tilted-up throughout.

Rebound kicking: Floating in the prone position, the swimmer uses his hands to push himself away from the wall feet-first. Then, with his arms still pointed ahead, he does one breaststroke kick to drive himself hands-first back to the wall. The cycle is repeated many times, the swimmer rebounding ever-farther from the wall, thus requiring more forceful kicks. The backward drift of the swimmer aids in cocking the feet high for the beginning of each kick.

Inverted kicking: With the arms together pointing the way, the swimmer kicks breaststroke on his back. This is useful in correcting, and making legal, the kick, and it also encourages the sought-after open angle of the thighs to the plane of the torso—which when done right side up amounts to a high catch of the feet. It blends in well as part of a larger sequence of drill-strokes. For example: Do crossed-wrist spearing (see above) on even-numbered lengths and inverted kicking on the odd—those with forward vision looking out for those on their backs.

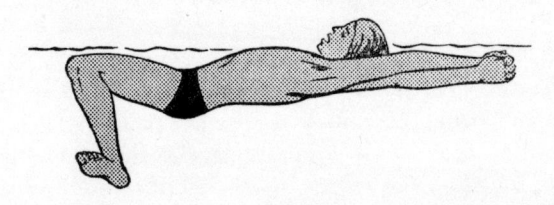

Underwater breaststroke: Although restricted in competition, it can be a rewarding training exercise. It can be done as a submerged version of the surface stroke, *i.e.* with the same arm movements and overall timing as the surface stroke, or it can be done using the pull-through-to-the-thighs arm action commonly used in the "pull-out" after a turn. The Soviet breaststroke squad which visited Canada in 1974 swam a large part of their workouts using the former method; in long, continuous swims they submerged for three strokes then returned to the surface for two, then submerged for three, and so on. This puts the swimmers in a constant state of oxygen debt, for one thing, but its main benefits are in the area of technique improvement and water awareness, *i.e.* "feel". The long-pull version is best used for short sprints of, say, 25 metres starting from a dive each time; it, too, is tiring, I suggest adequate periods of rest; the swimmers gain in self-confidence as they realize they *can* make the distance; and the skill itself figures in the one underwater stroke allowed at the beginning of each length in races. I find this drill helps *all* swimmers, especially butterflyers who can profit from learning how to drive themselves forward *through* the water.

A WORD OF CAUTION: It is *extremely dangerous* to go after underwater (without breathing) distance records; asphyxia can sneak up—the so-called "rapture of the deeps"—and render the best of swimmers unconscious.

Adjust-a-stroke: While swimming breaststroke, the swimmer

varies the size of his arm actions in progression according to a plan. For example: He may do a small stroke (hands barely separating), then a slightly larger stroke (about one-third the size of his usual stroke), then a larger one, and so on, working up to, and past, the size of stroke uses in straight breaststroke. The sequence is repeated over and over again while the swimmer, in effect, coaches himself, searching out the best size of arm action for him. Used in pre-competition warm-ups, it is especially beneficial.

Multi-parted drill sequences: Relief from boredom (always a problem) and stroke benefiting results are possible from the running together of various separate stroke drills. For example: Kick a 50, touching the ankles; then a 50 of crossed-wrists spearing; then a 50 of kicking while the hands take minute strokes well out in front; followed by a 50 of full-stroke but with the arm action greatly exaggerated; then swim a 50 of regular breaststroke; and repeat the cycle over and over non-stop; (this drill devised by U.S. Coach of the Year, Bob Miller, coach of the highly successful Colella brother-sister duo who won 1971 Pan Am Games breaststroke events). Almost any combination of parts, in sequence, will work, but thought should be given to the intended result. Even the simple sequence of legs-only followed by arms-only followed by full-stroke (which I have used for years, and in that order, *i.e.* with the arms-only immediately prior to full-stroke) repeated non-stop is good.

"Killer" drills: Some drills are notoriously taxing and therefore good as "conditioners" as well as skill developers. My favourite goes like this: The swimmers hold their hands out in front side by side, gliding, while they kick; after every third kick they blend in a normal arm pull; the cruncher is that they are permitted to breathe ONLY during the arm pull. So we have kick, kick, kick, pull-GASP, kick, kick, kick, pull-GASP, etc. The restriction on breathing forces good things; they kick faster—to get to the next breathing station; by the time they are permitted to breathe they are desperate for air and the accompanying arm action is executed smartly—which is as it should be in competition; and it serves to condition the large, oxygen-using muscles of the legs. I have found that the desired responses—desperate breathing, etc.—

show themselves best when the drill is sustained over moderately long swims of, say, 200 metres against time in sets of interval training repeats. It *is* a "killer". I have found the ratio of four-to-one to be too hard—it wiped out the majority of my squad. At times I have had groups do a set of twelve repeats, four at three-to-one, four at two-to-one, then four of regular, one-to-one breaststroke.

Belly-to-the-wall kicking: The swimmer holds himself as shown, belly to the wall, and executes the movements of the kick. It's a skill check a swimmer can give himself, not a conditioning drill. Between breaststroke repeat swims, for example, a swimmer may calmly do a little of this, while resting, as a reminder of the high catch and the alignment of the torso and thighs.

One-arm breaststroke: Use both legs but only one arm to swim breaststroke; the other arm trails at the side. This drill helps in selling the swimmers on the potential of the hands as sculling blades. Change arms each length. A real test, which when mastered can produce surprising speeds, is one-arm "arm(s)-only" breaststroke; with both legs and one arm "shut down", the swimmer sculls *vigorously* using small, very rapid back-and-forth motions of the hand and forearm well out in front. It's a little easier if the swimmer tilts to one side.

On breaststroke in general
It's sad, but "learn-to-swim" programmes in general—especially those locked into the use of manuals, "qualified" instructors,

examiners and elaborate systems of "proficiency" awards—are hopelessly out-of-date and stereotyped in their methods when it comes to breaststroke.

It's safe to say that a high percentage, if not all, of today's fastest breaststrokers would have trouble in getting a passing grade from the typical learn-to-swim examiner—so wide has the gulf become between those who seek pure efficiency and those who ignore efficiency in the interests of "style for style's sake".

I mention the above in the hope that parents and others who are of the old school, as it were, will refrain from interfering in the coaching of swimmers who compete today.

CHAPTER 5

Butterfly

Butterfly is such an esthetically satisfying stroke to swim it's a wonder it wasn't discovered sooner. True, it isn't a "utility stroke" —it isn't used in lifesaving, for example—but its flowing movements and induced sensations of exhilaration and power have an especial appeal to skilled swimmers. It is remarkable, for example, how many swimmers who have no serious ambitions in the stroke will swim butterfly upon first diving into the water at the beginning of a workout. "It just feels good."

I've found butterfly to be by far the most useful of the four strokes for general all-round training and conditioning. With the exception of the breaststroke kick, butterfly incorporates in one package all of the basic fundamentals and sophistications of the other strokes: bent-arm pull; water awareness (feel of the water); streamlining, good breathing habits; control; etc. Especially, it develops the major muscle groups used in freestyle and backstroke, and the carry-over of all these "goodies" to the other strokes is considerable—a phenomenon which isn't nearly so effective in reverse. A skilled butterflyer is much more likely to be also proficient in, say, freestyle than is a good freestyler likely to be good at butterfly. To train in butterfly amounts to training in three and one-half strokes (the front end of breaststroke benefits). In short, I believe that a squad that swims a lot of *good* butterfly in training is likely to be strong in all strokes.

For all that it has the reputation of being "that hard one", butterfly is *not* difficult once a swimmer learns to relax into the natural rhythm. The stroke looks hard to the uninitiated, and unfortunately it is the unskilled butterflyers who originate most of the adverse comments. We coaches don't help matters when we sometimes hold the threat of butterfly over our charges as a punishment for not fulfilling some other aspect of training.

Some imagine that the stroke requires great strength. Of course strength is always a factor in any athletic endeavour, but "flyers" need no more general strength than do other swimmers. Technique is of paramount importance, however. (Which perhaps explains why the good flyer, for whom skill is vital, usually finds the less-skill-demanding strokes relatively easy.)

When first taking up the stroke a swimmer is likely to "run out of air" or "be winded" after a short swim of, say, 25 metres. This is a special problem for butterfly novices. To be short of breath is not the same as being truly fatigued. The problem lies in a difficulty peculiar to the stroke. Most of the muscles used to execute the pull and then the double-arm recovery are attached or linked to the rib cage. When first learning the stroke the tendency is to tense all of the muscles of the torso in order to "murder the water" with poorly-directed, partly-downward strokes in an attempt to come high enough to flail the arms forward for each frantic stroke before wallowing again. This furious tensing of the entire torso effectively freezes the bellows-like action of the chest and diaphragm, and the struggling swimmer, in the throws of surviving, is soon winded.

Approached properly, the problem will soon pass. In the learning of butterfly there is a shortness-of-breath "barrier" that must be overcome. Once a swimmer learns to rhythmically relax and to regulate his breathing to fit naturally into the stroke cycle, longer and longer training swims can be handled with comparative ease.

Body position

The term *body position*, which pre-supposes the existence of some one more-or-less constant position of the torso, simply does not apply in butterfly swimming. A study of the stroke sequence drawings in this book will reveal this fact. However, some comment under this heading is in order.

In spite of the semblance of constant undulation of the whole of the body from head through to the feet, film studies of the best flyers show that the hips remain fairly constantly near the surface. The shoulders and head rise and fall above and below the surface with uninhibited abandon. The legs kick as a single unit, usually twice in each stroke-cycle. But the stroke fares better when the hips are kept up near, or at, the surface.

BUTTERFLY

In actual fact, I find it helps if the swimmer can think of the pivot point in the teeter-totter action as being farther down the body, not at the hips but at the centre of the thighs. Thus:

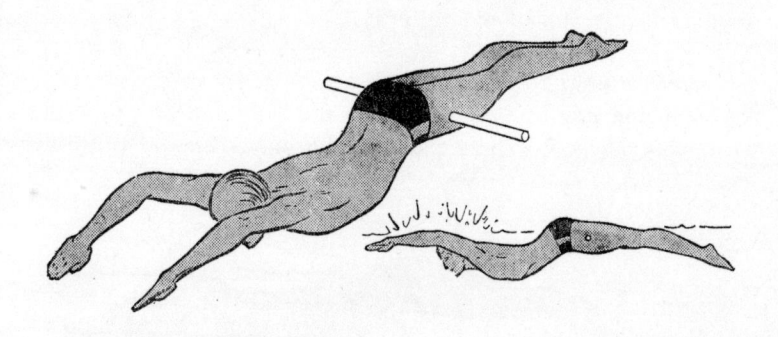

To get this across to swimmers I sometimes suggest that they imagine they are from another planet where the "humans" have their lungs not in their chests but in their thighs—that being the case, their thighs are buoyant while their chests, which are packed solid with muscle, tend to sink. This buoyant-thighs/non-floating-chest way of thinking promotes the desired sensation of swimming downhill, as if swimming down a fast-flowing river while the scenery whizzes by seemingly too fast for the effort expended.

The keeping of the hips and thighs high is difficult for beginners in the stroke. They are usually inept at getting their arms over the water if their hips are up; they tend to overdo the raising of their shoulders with the result that their hips and thighs sink, creating impossible amounts of drag. So, with virtually no momentum going for them, their attempts at stroking degenerate into floundering push-ups and splashings-down. Add to this mess their breathing difficulties (previously mentioned) and I have identified the main problems to be overcome when teaching the stroke: Keeping the hips and legs high (to reduce drag), and making breathing easier (survival).

Some dozen years ago I finally hit on what I believe is the simplest and best—and by far the most enjoyable—method of teaching-learning the modern butterfly stroke. This breakthrough came *after* many years of experimenting with the usual "stroke breakdown drills"—most of them arduous, some of them effective enough to contribute to the development of a five-time world record holder (Mary Stewart, 1962). I found a unique intermediate, or stepping-stone, adaptation of the butterfly stroke which poses few problems in breathing or in getting the hips and legs to ride high, all the while it exposes the swimmers to the slinky delights of true, full-blown butterfly.

One-arm butterfly
As the name implies, the swimmers use only one arm to stroke with while they otherwise perform the movements of butterfly.

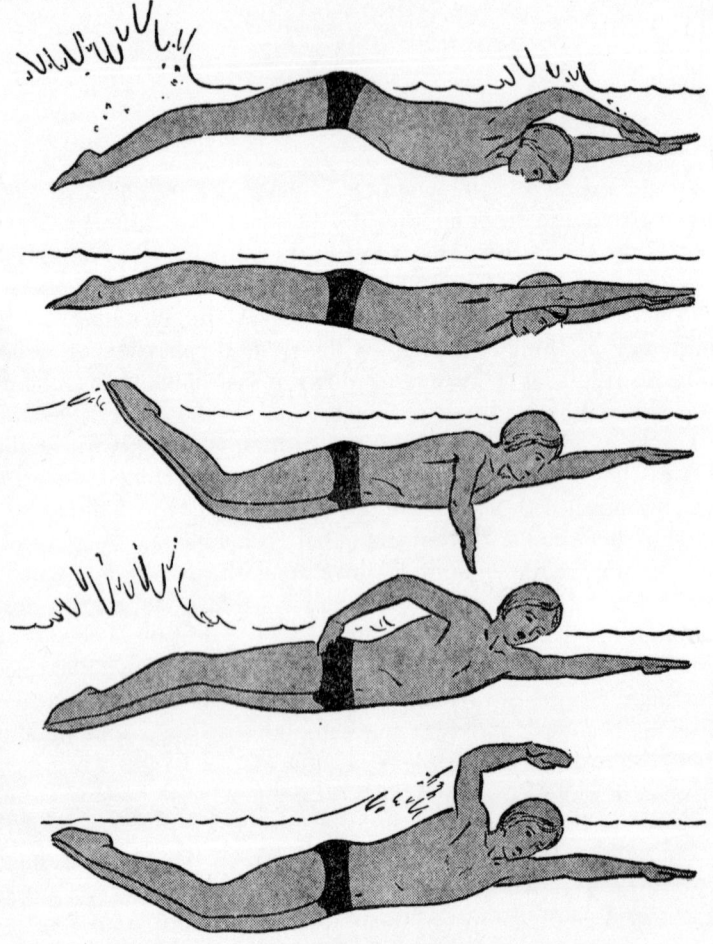

ONE-ARM BUTTERFLY SEQUENCE (arm in front)

BUTTERFLY

There are two basic styles of this intermediate stroke. In one, the swimmer keeps his unused arm out in front, spearing the way like a swordfish's sword. In the other style, the unused arm is kept loosely at the side. Both styles have their place in the teaching of butterfly but, of the two, I prefer the arm-spearing-the-way style for novice, intermediate, and some advanced butterfly pupils. It is more flowing, more controllable, and it lends itself better to variations which lead progressively into the full-blown stroke.

The stroke sequence begins with the swimmer prone in the water, gliding out from a push-off or dive. One arm remains out in front, spearing, as the other executes the pull-push of butterfly and comes out into the forward recovery swing. At this point the first advantages of this interim style become apparent, there is hardly any strain involved in executing the recovery, and the breath can be taken easily to the side (the entire body may tilt slightly upward to the side of the recovering arm, there is no harm in this), and the hips and thighs remain high in the water.

Next, the only crucial part of the sequence occurs. The swimmer should consciously bend his neck and direct his head and shoulders downward *into the water* in time with the re-entry of the easy-swinging hand and arm. This action is what it would be if the swimmer had to submerge cleanly, dolphin-like, in order to coast under a floating obstacle such as a log or canoe. In initiating this dive below, the swimmer should instinctively do a dolphin kick.

As the swimmer feels himself returning to the surface he begins the next stroke-cycle. His pulling hand eases into the "catch"; the arm shapes for the pull (bent-arm pull); and pulling pressure is applied in time with an unhurried raising of the head as the unused arm continues to spear, now slightly upward.

It's *vital* to this stroke—and to the butterfly stroke itself—that the pull start *before* the swimmer has returned his shoulders to the surface.

A tip for butterflyers: Pull to come up, don't come up to pull.

This point is most important. The butterflyer who dips below in time with his hand entry and then delays the start of the next pull until after his shoulders have returned to the surface (where they encounter significantly more resistance) will almost invariably rip his arms through the water with much waste of effort; worse, he'll not experience the *flow* of the total stroke experienced by those who do it right. Ideally, the hands and arms should not move backwards through the water; the body should be pulled past the anchored-in-the-water arms. This desired arrangement is more likely to occur when the pull is started while the swimmer is still submerged and in the upslope phase of his glide under that imaginary floating obstacle. I sometimes tell my swimmers to ram *through* the water as they would if they were intending to butt, or ram, a hole in a boat below the waterline. The mastery of this subtle difference in the timing of the pull can knock gratifying chunks off a butterflyer's best time. I find that the one-arm interim stroke helps in getting this subtle point through to the pupils better than any other drill.

The leg action is, of course, the dolphin kick. Because of the tilt of the body, the kick may angle slightly to the side, which is all right—the water doesn't know the difference. What does matter is that the swimmer learns to time his kicks so they occur at the logical moments in the overall stroke cycle.

In butterfly, the accepted norm is two kicks per stroke cycle. It's not a legislated rule, it has just worked out to that rhythm after countless thousands of butterflyers have logged still more countless hours and miles of the stroke. It's the natural ratio; swimmers who deviate from it are handicapping themselves.

The usual approach to the teaching of the kicks is to say that one kick happens as the hands enter the water and that the other happens as the push is ending—and that, in fact, is based on the truth. But I've found that a surprising number of swimmers—including a couple of my world record holders—simply don't know precisely where their hands are as they stroke. Their attempts at timing the kicks relative to the hand movements frequently result in frustration-charged sessions with the swimmers wanting desperately to learn, often with much disappointing trial-and-erroring. Some never really getting the hang of it.

I've found it much simpler, and infinitely more satisfactory, to have my swimmers relate the timing of the kicks to the movements of the head. The head is, after all, the "top bone" in the linkage. It is, in a manner of speaking, the "handle of the whip"; its movements can trigger the kicks directly, and on cue. I simply tell my swimmers to kick once when the head goes down, and to kick again when the head comes up. It works! It's *natural* and it's *second nature* (with a little conscious help).

BUTTERFLY

The one-arm butterfly is so free of strain that the novice who learns to lower his head each time his hand enters will instinctively feel an urge to kick just at that moment. The second kick—the one which happens as the head comes up—usually needs some coaxing from the coach; in fact, sometimes it needs a lot of coaxing, but the results are worth it.

Most beginners will swim faster with one-arm butterfly than they can with the double-arm stroke; they can go faster with half the arm-power. The reason is simple: The higher position of the afterparts of the body allows for better streamlining, *i.e.* less drag. It's so much easier with one-arm butterfly to maintain a reasonable speed that almost from the beginning it is possible to handle longer swims. This, in turn, allows the swimmers to log practice lengths while experiencing the proper rhythms, etc.

This interim, one-arm stroke is fun to swim, veteran butterflyers enjoy it and recognize its value. Quite on their own, for example, they are likely to use it as part of their warming-up routine for a race. It "grooves in" their racing stroke.

Variations

The basic one-arm stroke, described above, involves using the same arm over and over again for a length of the pool and then changing to the other arm for the next length, and so on. But there are many variations, each of them enjoyable, each serving to advance the butterfly skill-learning process.

Some of the variations I have used, and still rely on, are as follows:

(1) *Three-length cycle:* Swim the first length using right arm, swim the second length using left arm and swim the third length using both arms (regular butterfly); repeat cycle over and over as desired.

(2) *Three and three:* Swim first three *strokes* using the right arm only, swim second three strokes using only the left; then three right, three lefts; and so on. (A variation of this is *two and two*.)

NOTE: The changing of arms "on the go" is not difficult when the unused arm remains in front. The swimmer returns to the both-arms-in-front position briefly after each stroke, which allows the change-over to be accomplished smoothly and with no break in the total rhythm. In fact this change-over not only reduces tedium, it gives the swimmer valuable experience in the timing of the subtle beginning movements of his arm strokes. The carry-over of this all-important skill into the full-blown butterfly—and for that matter, into *all* of the four strokes—is considerable.

(3) *Three-two-one-full stroke:* A four-length drill. Swim first length doing three rights, three lefts, three rights, etc.; swim second length doing two and two; for the third length it's right, change, left, change, etc.; length four is done in regular butterfly; repeat cycle as desired.

(4) *Uno-uno-dos:* (One-one-two in Spanish.) Do a right-arm stroke and return to the both-arms-in-front "point" position, then a left-arm stroke and return to the point, then a double-arm stroke (regular butterfly for one stroke), and repeat the cycle over and over. I hit on this variation a few years before the Mexico City Olympic Games, hence its Spanish name.

NOTE: This is an example of the giving of special names to the many, many drills and variations of drills in order to save time when calling out workout changes.

(5) *Uno-dos-uno-dos:* Similar to (4) above. Swim one stroke with the right arm, one with *both* arms, one with the left, then one with both arms, and so on. Other variations on this theme are: *Uno-uno-dos-dos*; *uno-uno-dos-dos-dos*; *uno-dos-dos*; etc.

NOTE: This introducing of frequent double-arm strokes bridges the gap between the pure one-arm style and the true racing butterfly.

(6) *Three-two-one-change:* A novelty drill with a purpose. Swim *three* strokes with the right arm; *two* with the left; then *one* with the right; now three with the *left*; two with the right; one with the right; and so on. (RRR-LL-R-LLL-RR-L, etc.)

NOTE: The mental challenge of keeping the counts right adds zest.

(7) *Three-two-one-complete the length full-stroke:* From the push-off swim the first three strokes with the right, then two

BUTTERFLY

with the left, then one with the right, then swim regular butterfly for the remainder of the length; swim each succeeding length in the same manner.

NOTE: The one-arm portion at the beginning of each length serves to review the rhythm before the swimmer goes into full-stroke butterfly.

I suggest that the coach-reader come up with a few variations of his own, perhaps giving them his own pet names.

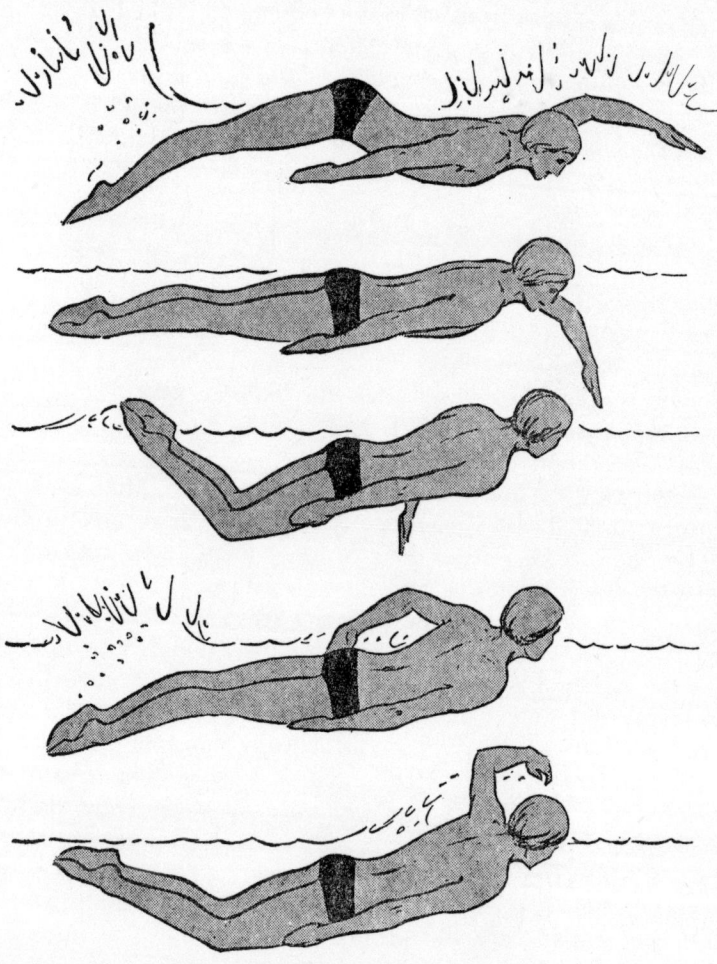

ONE-ARM BUTTERFLY (arm at side)

The second style of basic one-arm butterfly sees the unused arm at the side. This version doesn't lend itself as readily to variations, but it incorporates more of the uninhibited action of the aggressive, international brand of butterfly. With no resting arm out in front there is virtually no stabilizing support of the head and shoulders. With each forward swing of an arm, the front end of the torso crashes down through the surface. The chain-reaction effect thus induced pikes the hips abruptly upward and an instinctive dolphin kick explodes downward.

As in the arm-in-front style, the body may be tilted slightly to one side, and the in-and-out action of the head can trigger the precise timing of the two dolphin kicks of each stroke.

I use both kinds of basic one-arm butterfly in my coaching. Further: I have often used one or the other on particular individuals in order to bring about specific desirable alterations in technique.

There is a third type of interim butterfly stroke:

Dive-stroke butterfly
I've heard this called many names but "dive-stroke butterfly" is the most descriptive. This is the stroke used by many in competition in the first few years after the "dolphin fishtail" butterfly was legislated into recognition as a separate competitive stroke in 1952. World records were set with it.

The swimmer uses both arms simultaneously. After each recovery, he deliberately makes a deeper than usual re-entry dive below the surface, deeper than for the modern racing stroke, that is—to a depth of two or three feet for adults, somewhat less for youngsters. Once below, the swimmer keeps his arms out in front while he executes several outsized, full-body undulations, emulating the action of a dolphin. The rhythm is not at all hurried. The swimmer slides along below for perhaps two or three of his own bodylengths experiencing an esthetically satisfying at-oneness with "Mother Water". After three or four or more semi-lazy dolphin-like undulations the swimmer aims his body slightly upward and begins an arm pull so timed as to explode out into a butterfly arm recovery and breath. The arms are swung over the water in a slow, ponderous way, a breath is taken, and then the swimmer literally dives hands first below the water again.

Done well, it's a beautiful stroke to watch. The viewer is

reminded of the nobility of ponderously powerful whales. The swimmer's feet come out of the water, much as the tail planes (flukes) of a whale do, and linger, poised momentarily as the whole of the body glides smoothly forward and downward below the surface. The feet slide under, almost as an after-thought, through the same "hole" in the surface used by the rest of the body.

An experienced swimmer of average ability should have no trouble in cruising lengths of a 50-metre pool averaging eight to ten strokes per length.

Dive-stroke butterfly, bestowing as it does a profound awareness of the fundamental nature of swimming on an individual, is good for all swimmers, not only butterflyers. The stroke is ideal for cruising swimming during periods of relaxation between sets of interval training. It's fun! Perhaps better than any other drill, it imparts the sought-after *feel* of swimming. It's a pity it isn't a separate competitive stroke in its own right; spectators and swimmers alike would enjoy it.

In a manner of speaking, butterfly is an "honest" stroke in that its every movement is necessary to the whole—just as in classic chess problems (the kind seen regularly in many daily newspapers) every piece on the board has a reason for being there, so is butterfly "pure", *i.e.* there are no unnecessary frills. It *is* surprising that the stroke wasn't discovered sooner, and it isn't surprising that it now enjoys such popularity.

Butterfly arm action

As the arms enter the water for the beginning of a new stroke they should be slightly bent at the elbows, the bony tips of the elbows angled upward. At the moment of hand entry, the elbows and forearms should be higher than the rapidly submerging shoulders and head. In fact the elbows and forearms should be the *last* to submerge as the front end of the swimmer is tipped forward and in. The hands, which enter at about shoulder width or slightly wider, should be rotated about 45 degrees from the horizontal, thumbside downmost.

The whole arrangement of the upper body, upper arms, elbows, forearms and hands is one of grotesque distortion and exaggeration. It doesn't occur in any other activity I know of, yet it is vital to the success of butterfly (and to breaststroke, and one arm at a time, to freestyle and backstroke as well). The deltoid muscles—the rounded muscles which cap the shoulders—are rolled inward toward the cheeks. The shoulderblades swing outward across the back and jut outward visibly. The upperarms rotate upward, the tips of the elbows uppermost and higher than the top of the head. I'll say again that as the whole of the body forward of the hips goes underwater the elbows and forearms are the last to submerge, and even then they remain just below the surface as the swimmer feels for the "catch" of the new pull.

To teach this, I show films, demonstrate with my plasticine man, draw pictures on my poolside blackboard, but especially I have the swimmers actually experience it on the deck.

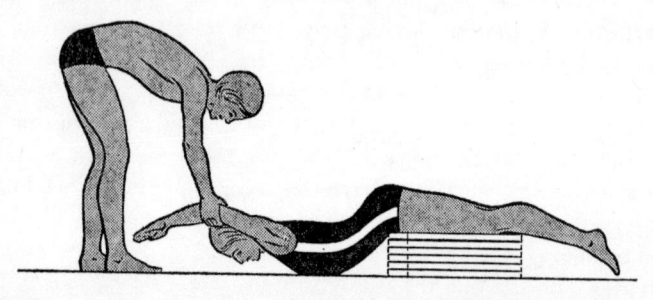

I have them take turns lying prone, as illustrated, with their hips and thighs resting on a stack of, say, four kickboards and their chests on the deck while a partner pulls their bent elbows upward, creating for them the distorted shape I am after. In the course of regular workouts, I will frequently have these "stroke review stations", *i.e.* stacks of kickboards, here and there on the deck so that the swimmers may, with the aid of a partner, check out the feeling for themselves from time to time between training swims.

In the water, once the entry has been made, there is a brief pause as the swimmer feels for the catch. I've found that this searching-out of the catch is best done, surprisingly, with a slight *upward* movement of the hands and arms. At least that is the sensation they should experience—as if a cannon ball were to be suddenly dropped squarely between their shoulder-blades just as the entry is made. (Such a solid impact from above would drive the chest downward and cause a reflexive upward action of the arms and hips.)

The first part of the pull is "low key", *i.e.* soft—like the touch of a skilled pickpocket. There is no strain involved in the pull as the arms separate as if to make room for the rest of the body to move between them, driven forward by its own considerable momentum. I can't stress this "soft" beginning of the pull enough; more than anything else, it is the mark of the gifted butterflyer. As this soft catch is firming up into a solid purchase on the water there is a *slight* pause in the rhythm of the double-dolphin kick: For a moment the legs are kept streamlined and high in the water —as if stunned into inactivity by the impact of that cannon ball I spoke of.

Definitely, the swimmer should avoid the common butterfly flaw of wrenching abruptly at the water at the beginning of the pull (or at any other point in the pull for that matter).

The hands perform mainly as sculling blades throughout most of the pull. From the entry they sweep outward as the forearms are pressed downward by a rotating of the upper arms at the shoulders. The elbows remain high in the water until they are spread wide in line with the forehead. (At this point the swimmer is altering the direction of his momentum-charged head and shoulders upward through the surface.) As the action continues, the hands and forearms, which have rounded the widest part of the pull, begin to move inward. The arms, which should have about a 95° bend at the elbows, are then brought downward and inward, each pivoting as a unit from the shoulder socket. The hands are brought in under the swimmer to where they are a handlength apart near the waist. From this point the hands move outward again into an abbreviated push. The recovery begins with the hands abandoning pushing and clearing the water little-finger-side first about even with the legband of the swim suit.

Contrary to what many coaches still preach (and would like to believe, apparently), the successful butterflyers simply do *not* push all the way to "full extension" of the arms rearward below the surface. Their elbows, according to filmed evidence, do not straighten out in the water at the end of the push.

To teach the *natural* length of the pull-push, I have my swimmers sit on a bench or the edge of the pool and touch their fingertips to the top of the bench, or the deck, beside their hips. As you sit reading this you might try it yourself, note the angle of the elbows.

For each swimmer there is a right length of pull-push which blends into the rhythm of his total stroke—and into the wave patterns he creates. The pull-push that is too short or too long disrupts the rhythm.

In butterfly, rhythm—the "marrying" of the parts to the whole—is of the utmost importance, just as "stride" is to a runner.

Not only is the moderate length of the pull-push best for the rhythm, it leads into a recovery action which reduces strain on the shoulder muscles and on the workings of the shoulder-joint itself. The turning of the palms toward the hips just prior to the start of the recovery aids in getting the elbows up early which in turn circumvents an awkward binding of the shoulder-joint which plagues those who insist on using the once-popular straight-arm recovery.

The action at the end of the push and beginning of the recovery reminds me of the "fast draw" of old-time western "gunfighters". The bent elbows, the turned hands (as if to grip the butts of six-guns), and the slightly-hunched shoulders are right out of a "Western" movie. And remember, the actors are re-enacting a "life and death" skill—not performing some theoretically "correct" style.

I suspect that this type of recovery-beginning developed more as a matter of straight survival than because of any wisdom of coaches. It is what the young, weak swimmers used to do before they were "strong enough" to use the once-standard, coach-devised, straight-arm recovery of a decade or so ago. Now, because of the massive workouts many flyers are exposed to, swimmers have fallen naturally into what works best—even though a surprising number of their coaches are still paying lip-service to the old notions about pushing all the way to full extension.

The arms should be relaxed at the wrists and elbows as they swing forward over the water. The keeping of the elbows bent shortens the length of the arms and reduces muscle strain, and, with the arms thus shortened, faster, more accurate movements are possible. A number of today's best butterflyers, especially those blessed with superior flexibility, execute what is virtually a double freestyle recovery with their elbows high and their hands and forearms relatively close to the body. For those who use an essentially straight-arm recovery, I find it helps correct timing problems if the extremities of the arms—the hands and forearms—are independently speeded forward as if the elbows were to encounter vertical obstacles such as slender posts thereby forcing a wrap-around acceleration of the hands just prior to re-entry. A pure straight-arm recovery demands unusual strength in the deltoid and upper-back muscles and, in addition, asks too much in the accuracy department—just as it is unreasonable to ask a person to write at a blackboard with a totally straight arm, so is it unreasonable to expect precision of timing and accuracy of a stiff-arm recovery.

The recovery, for all that it can be classified as a "neutral" aspect of the stroke—it is not a movement against water, for example—should receive conditioning attention from the coach. The muscles which execute the recovery are just as prone to fatigue as the pulling muscles, and when the recovery muscles give out the whole stroke suffers. If this seems of little importance to the reader, I dare him to stand and bend over at the waist and then take the arms through the ideal limb track of the full stroke for a minute or two. It is *not* easy, yet we coaches, caught up as we are in the positive aspects of the stroke—pulling, kicking, etc.—seldom give the lowly recovery muscles the conditioning they need. Serious butterfly swimmers should be exposed to a lot of high-repetition/low-resistance pulley weight or similar exercises to "train up" the muscles of the upper back (between the shoulder-blades). With these muscles equipped to handle the problem, butterfly can become "butter-FLIT", and 100s and 200s become considerably easier. I can't stress this aspect enough: far too many butterflyers break down in competition because of poorly conditioned recovery "prime movers". This is the weakest link in most butterfly training programmes.

Pulls: Keyhole v. Hourglass
From the way the two terms, "keynote pull" and "hourglass pull", are used indiscriminately—often by the best-known coaches—one might suppose they apply to the same thing. I prefer to think of them as being related but rather different in character.

The keyhole pull is so named because the hands during the pull trace the outline of an outsized keyhole shape: They start relatively close together, move outward and around, come almost together again at what might be termed the "waist" of the keyhole and then they move slightly outward again.

The hourglass pull is similar but the hands are already as far apart as the widest part of the keyhole tracing when they enter; there is virtually no additional spreading apart of the hands at the start of the pull. From the entry the hands move inward and then outward, tracing the outline of a large hourglass.

The keyhole pull, in my opinion, is the better of the two and is by far the more generally used. It allows the swimmer to enjoy his momentum as he takes that brief, streamlined pause to search out the *feel* of the "catch"; the hourglass pull, in comparison, because of its wide letter "Y" entry, requires an immediate grasping rip at the water to offset the tendency for the sprawled arms to effectively, and rather abruptly, perform as brakes. The hourglass swimmer, broadly speaking (no pun intended), is obliged to descend his hands from the recovery into the pull with no pausing for the "catch"; it is definitely a non-gliding form of butterfly, which must please coaches with "no glide in butterfly" fixed in their brains; but it is a foolishly costly form of butterfly. The slap-dash pulls of the typical hourglass flyer remind me of the so-called "slap-shot" used in ice hockey.

There is more "run", or "flow" to the keyholer's swimming. And this prompts me to discuss a facet of swimming which is seldom given proper consideration by coaches and swimmers alike, momentum, or, if you prefer, inertia.

A 150-pound swimmer weighs about 1/13th of a ton! (I often have my swimmers figure out their weight in fractions of a ton.) If he were to be modelled in wood, as a statue, and propelled at his usual swimming speed, the pool management wouldn't allow him in the pool; he would smash tiles at the ends, for one thing, not to mention the lethal menace he would be to other swimmers. If our 150-pound swimmer moves through the water at a rate of five feet per second (the speed of one minute for 100 yards) he has inertia to the tune of 750 foot-pounds per second. In outer space, where there is virtually no resistance, this inertia would keep him moving long past our lifetime. But in the pool, the resistance of the water is real, the *slightest* imperfection in alignment, in streamlining, can add to this resistance, which in turn can run up the elapsed time on a stop watch.

The typical hourglass swimmer reminds me of a car moving at

high speed in low gear. The slightest let-up on the accelerator and the braking power of the engine takes charge instantly, slowing the car's speed. I prefer to have my swimmers operate in what might be compared to high gear, or overdrive in a car. They always start off from the beginning of each length with full momentum, imparted by the dive or the push-off, so their task is merely one of maintaining that momentum. Done right, they have no need for low gears, they are catapulted into the start of each length, launched directly into the high- or overdrive range of gears, as it were. Brute power, the power to start from a dead stop—such as is essential in water polo—is not necessary when a swimmer learns to use his momentum effectively. Scientists have determined that the great whales require only about forty horsepower, so efficient are they at utilizing their momentum. If a swimmer is to achieve even part of the grace of sea creatures such as dolphins, he must learn that speed is not all a matter of applied force. Once he masters the use of streamlining and momentum he can cruise at race speeds with economy of effort and with much lower stroke rates. It goes further than that with butterfly. It is most unlikely that swimmers who are unmindful of the subtleties of streamlining and momentum will ever make it as good sprinters. I have observed that amongst the "bullwork", oblivious-to-momentum type of butterflyers—many of them hourglass pullers—their best times over 100 metres is often their split time on the way to a 200, and that has to indicate something, they are "grinders"—not "swimmers". They are to be pitied; they "don't hear the music". They are robots!

Also, the butterflyer who uses the wide-entry, hourglass type of pull is less likely to be a better-than-average freestyler. Just as in his butterfly, the hourglass swimmer will almost invariably take an excessive number of strokes per length—"spinning his wheels". Which is another reason why I prefer the keyhole pull over the hourglass variety with my swimmers.

With each form of pull there are many variations in the "limb tracks" used.

In general, the more powerful swimmers sweep their hands wider for longer and guide them close together late in the pull—at about the line of the bottom ribs; weaker flyers tend to bring their hands close together relatively early in the pull—sometimes as early as the line of the forehead—and then push directly rear-ward along parallel paths for the remainder of the pull-push. There have been, however, powerfully-built successful international butterflyers who have used the "weakling's pull"; my conjecture is that in their case it was a matter of having started that way as youngsters and through years of training their strengths developed specifically to match their movements. (This phenomenon of "specificity" in this case points out the need for acquiring the best possible technique early in each swimmer's career.)

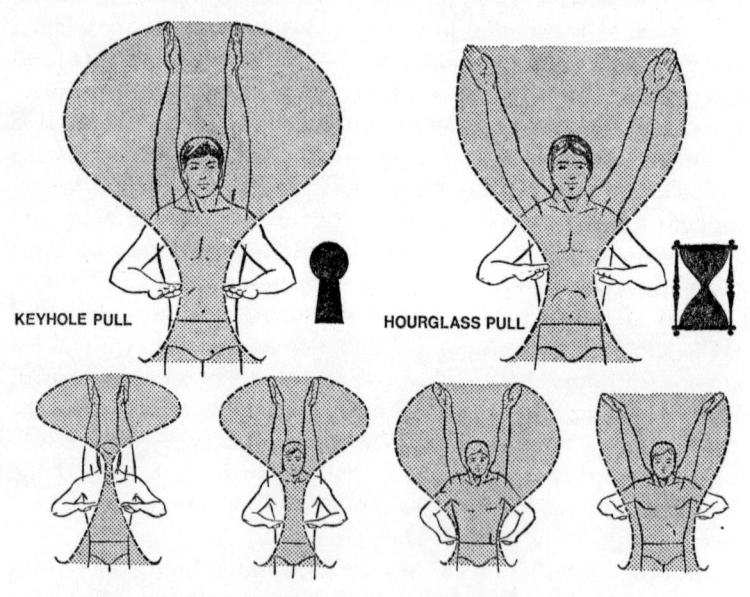

THE KEYHOLE PULL AND THE HOURGLASS PULL

Dr. James E. Counsilman, of Indiana University, and one of the great investigative coaches, has shown conclusively through the use of cinema photography—most of which he shoots himself, sometimes from the bottom of the pool—that, with the best swimmers, much of the thrust or pulling power derived from the hands in the butterfly pull (and in the pulls of the other strokes as well) results from a blade-like sculling action outward (keyhole pull) then inward and then outward again.

The best swimmers hit on this, probably quite unconsciously, years ago. The action is natural, it feels comfortable and, happily, it complies with the fundamental laws of fluid mechanics. A maximum of thrust (lift) is derived from a minimum of expended effort, hence the keyhole and hourglass pulls.

I strongly recommend that all swimmers—not just butterflyers—be exposed to regular sessions of pure sculling with the hands—the kind of sculling used so skilfully by synchronized swimmers. Most of what we erroneously call the pull in all strokes is primarily a sculling action.

One last comment on the arm action; the swimmer should *not* be able to see his hands as the arms complete the recovery and re-enter the water. The head should go about its business and lower the face as the torso descends taking the eyes below the surface while the arms are still in the air.

Beginners tend to keep their heads and shoulders too high too long; they tend to watch their hands splash down. This delay in lowering the head effectively stifles the desired action of the body; the hips and thighs remain too deep.

To counter this tendency, I find it helps if the swimmers try not to look at *anything* in detail. It takes our eyes a moment to focus on a new target, especially if we have just lifted them out of water and there is still water running off. That moment of waiting to be able to see can destroy the continuity of the stroke. So I sometimes tell my swimmers to keep their eyes sleepily out-of-focus as they swim. A subtle trick, but a most effective one.

Leg action

It's safe to say that any swimmer would complain bitterly if prior to an important butterfly race the referee were to tell him that the others are allowed to kick but that he must swim arms-only. Put that way, it would be distressing indeed, but countless would-be butterflyers swim as if such an edict had been pronounced against them.

"Lazy-leggers," I call them.

There should be two kicks in the complete butterfly cycle. The cycle isn't complete if both are not exploited to the fullest. But the kicks perform different functions. The one that happens as the arms reach forward for their "catch" (in time with the lowering of the head) is primarily a ruddering action, I call it a "squash kick" in that it is directed more downward than backward, the better to tip the front end of the swimmer into the water and to bring off the desired totally streamlined alignment of his whole body. To properly evaluate the importance of this, the reader should know that the highest speeds ever attained in swimming, in terms of feet per second, are those measured during the "flying" part of butterfly. The swimmer surges forward and partly over the water having used all four of his limbs at once. He has more momentum going for him at that moment than at any other time. It would be folly for him to do other than "land" cleanly and pierce through the water, certainly it would not help if he were to flex his knees excessively—applying brakes as it were—in a futile attempt to further propel himself. To do so would negate his actions which led up to his exploding out into the recovery and re-entry phase of the stroke. The second kick, the one which coincides with the last half of the arm pull, and the one which helps in driving the swimmer up to that high speed mentioned above, should be more propulsive. This kick involves what for beginners seems like an exaggerated bending of the knees—most beginners have difficulty in believing that the coach wants such an exaggerated action. The entire action of this second kick, from legs streamlined through the bend, kick and back to legs streamlined again (in time to enjoy that high-speed "flying" sensation), is swift and whiplike. The feet clear the water as they come forward (less drag) prior to being smashed down and backward causing a distinctive and characteristic plum of water to fly into the air just as the hands are lifted into the arm recovery.

This second kick, along with the conservation of momentum previously discussed, is essential to world-class sprint butterfly. Note that the kick comes into play in time to assist the arms in driving the swimmer forward. I liken the relationship of the two, pulling and kicking this second kick, to the situation where a person is trying to pull himself up to the top of a high fence—the receiving of "a boost up" from a friend on the ground would be a distinct advantage at such a time, the climber's arms wouldn't have to work nearly as hard as they would if the operation was one of strictly "arms only".

Add to the picture the fact that our thigh muscles are perhaps the strongest we have, and that our feet and lower legs can serve admirably as propelling surfaces, and it becomes indeed ridiculous to not use them in what is, or should be, a surging, maximum-effort activity.

In executing both types of kick, it helps if the knees are allowed to spread slightly—a few inches—as they bend, it's even an advantage to be slightly bowlegged. It is definitely an advantage to be able to bend the knees forward, beyond the straight, *i.e.* to have hyperextension of the knees (Mark Spitz's successes were aided in this way) but I know of no exercises to promote this, and it is probably ill-advised, medically, to attempt to "improve" on Nature in this regard.

With youngsters, it only confuses things to ask them to differentiate between the two types of kick; I simply tell them to make both kicks feel the same in size and effort and let the rhythm of the stroke itself lead them into the right uses of the kicks.

Breathing patterns
For nearly two decades now it has been the standard practice of most coaches to instruct their butterflyers to breathe "every other stroke". I followed this line myself. The thinking was that the raising of the head and shoulders high enough to accomplish a breath detracted from the effectiveness of the stroke in the streamlining department so I, for one, used to tell my swimmers to "come up for air then stay down for a good one (pull)", *i.e.* skip every other opportunity to breathe in favour of obtaining more thrust, less drag, and greater distance during the non-breathing stroke. I had some successes, six world records and a dozen national titles, including three American Championship wins. (For the record, most of the swimmers in those races did breathe every other stroke.)

So standard was this "double breathing" (a misnomer) that when Olympic and other major races were won by swimmers who breathed more often—some, every stroke—their breathing patterns were dismissed as "exceptions to the rule".

Today, more and more butterflyers are being coached to breathe "when they feel like it". It is now recognized that the raising of the shoulders and head in each stroke-cycle can be beneficial to the total action. The swimmer might as well breathe.

(The abandonment of "double breathing" was achieved years ago in breaststroke; it's surprising that it took so long for butterfly theorists to get the message.)

The foregoing notwithstanding, most modern butterfly swimmers breathe more or less according to some predetermined plan, depending on the race distance and pool size. Some breathe only three or four times during the first quarter of a 100—especially in a short pool—then more often, perhaps every other stroke, for the middle part of the race, and then more often still for the last quarter. Others will reverse that pattern. So it goes on, each using a breathing pattern in which he has confidence. Mark Spitz favoured taking three breaths then skipping one then three more,

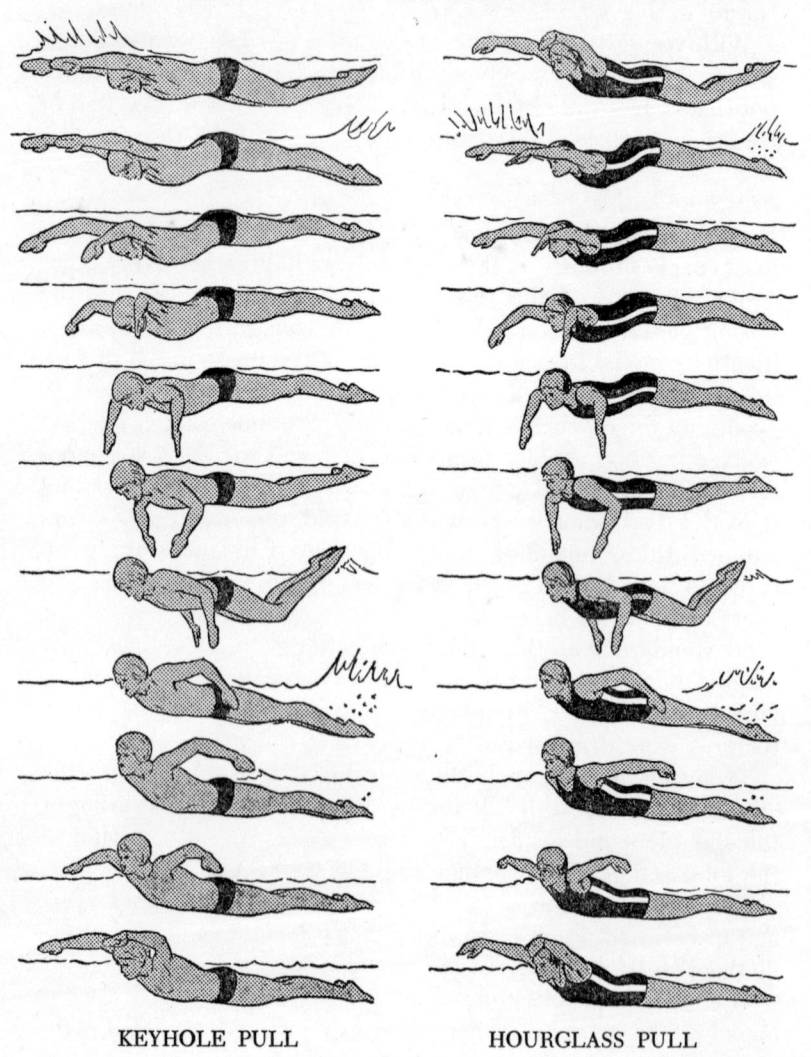

KEYHOLE PULL   HOURGLASS PULL

and so on. Many outstanding "200 men" have breathed on every stroke throughout.

Head position
One almost never sees a top butterflyer breathing to the side any more, although it was once popular, especially with Australians during the '50s and early '60s. Again, the thinking was that it would allow the head to remain lower, thus minimizing the deviation of the body from the "ideal" (many thought) level position. Now we know that the raising of the head straight to the front reduces the constriction of the "pipes" of the throat (as in mouth-to-mouth resuscitation), and, anyway, it helps to induce the propulsive action of the body from the waist rearward.

Beginners should raise and lower their heads noticeably, as described earlier, and continue to do so as they become more proficient. However, there are many polished flyers who keep their heads poised in a constant attitude, face forward, relative to the torso, but they raise and submerge their heads on cue, *i.e.* it is still the "top bone" in the linkage.

In summation
Swimmers and coaches alike should approach butterfly with a positive attitude, recognizing that the stroke is to general swimming ability what vitamins are to health.

CHAPTER 6

Wave Patterns

Many a romantic ocean traveller has gazed at the wake of a cruise ship, probably never realizing the tell-tale information such waves can convey in regard to the design and characteristics of the ship.

Naval airmen have long been taught to identify from great altitude the size, class, and speed of ships by reading their wave patterns.

Similarly, when the best swimmers swim they create distinctive wave patterns that differ markedly from those of mediocre swimmers. The knowledgeable observer can read the various wave patterns and use the information thus gained to gauge the effectiveness of each swimmer's technique. A coach may note, for example, the characteristics of the pattern created when a swimmer is going well and use that information at a future time when there is a need to "tune up" that swimmer's stroke.

An entire book could be devoted to this fascinating aspect of swimming coaching, yet, to my knowledge, I have been alone in my use of wave patterns as an aid to coaching.

Once a coach begins to pay attention to the character of the waves his swimmers create, a whole new dimension in stroke analysis and correction is opened to him. Just as a mechanic may make an adjustment when tuning up an engine and then refer to patterns visually displayed on an oscilloscope, so may the knowledgeable coach make an adjustment in a swimmer's technique and then refer to the wave patterns that result.

Upon seeing an outstanding swimmer perform, a coach may record in his mind the *total* of the images he sees. The actual movements, etc., of the stroke *and* the wave pattern that is intrinsically part of the whole—the better to convey his findings to his swimmers.

I've found that even subtle adjustments in the arch of the back, the position of the head, the length of the push, the timing of the stroke, etc., can bring about profound changes in the wave patterns.

When a good swimmer's stroke "turns sour" (when he is trying as hard as ever, or harder, but with disappointing results) the chances are that the problem will manifest itself in the form of altered wave patterns.

Since no two swimmers are exactly alike in strengths, dimensions, displacements (a nautical term), and technique, even the best have patterns uniquely their own at least in some small detail. Since their waves are created by their movement through the water, variations in swimming speed loom as a significant factor to be considered—the same swimmer at different speeds will produce different patterns.

This last, I am sure, will become increasingly more important in the training of swimmers. Some explanation is in order, now that many coaches have nearly reached the practical limits of daily time they can ask a swimmer to devote to in-the-water training, it must become a matter of making the available time more productive if we are to see continued improvement. In other words, if we can't train longer, we must train more wisely. When a training swimmer merely cruises at, say, 80 per cent of his potential speed—which is what most swimmers on high-mileage programmes tend to do *in order to survive*—the waves he creates differ considerably from those he will make at full speed in a race. I see in this a serious flaw in the currently-popular super-mileage approach to swimming training.

Frankly, I have always preferred to train my swimmers as much as possible at or near race speeds, using shorter swims if need be—especially once I began to appreciate the wave-pattern phenomena.

I'm convinced that at race speeds the best swimmers are married to, *and assisted by*, the living waves they create. I use the word *living* advisedly in as much that a wave, once created, has a "life" of its own. The swell of a wave and the trough between waves can fit around a swimmer and actually help carry him along or, at least, make his task easier.

Olympic paddlers and oarsmen refer to getting their boats "up" as soon as possible after a start. They strive to get their boats up to a speed where a feeling of easy-riding takes hold. Similarly, skilled pleasure craft sailors know the importance of proper weight distribution in order to "trim" a boat so that its hull fits, or is cradled, in its own waves. They can *feel* when their boat is "at one" with its waves.

And so it can be with swimmers. They can't avoid making waves; they might as well make "good" ones.

I'll say it again: The effort a coach puts into learning to "read" wave patterns can make him a better coach.

I won't attempt to describe or illustrate all of the possible variations in wave patterns. Rather, I will comment on only a few of the more obvious things to look for. In the final analysis, the reader-coach who wants to use this extra dimension will have to educate himself, studying from the real thing; he must develop a practised eye.

Breaststroke waves
The position of the "bow wave", relative to the head, can serve as a useful guide in assessing the efficiency of the overall timing of the stroke. This wave, once created, has a forward momentum

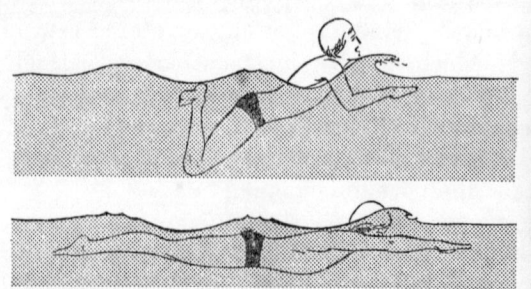

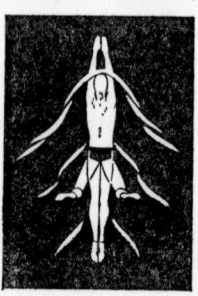

of its own. If the swimmer is constantly moving up to it only to fall behind it again on each stroke, as if the bow wave is repeatedly getting away from him, it indicates that he is not progressing smoothly and steadily. Something is wrong! Either the legs are not taking over from the arms on cue, or vice versa, or it could be that there is excessive drag involved at some point in the action. As stated earlier, the coach may tinker with the stroke until the telltale wave patterns show that the problem has been resolved.

At full speed, there are two dominant waves. The bow wave that normally emanates from a point a few inches in front of the face, and a second V-like wave that originates at the hips. Following each wave there is a trough where the water dips below the normal level of the surface. The first trough exposes the swimmer's back when he rises for a breath. This can be a guide, and depending on the style of breaststroke the coach prefers, the exposure of the backs of the upper arms (seen best from the rear) in time with the taking of a breath can be noted also.

Without realizing it, some world-class breaststrokers and their coaches make use of the second trough as a guide. At race speeds this trough dips to its lowest just above where the drawn-up feet are cocked into their "high catch" attitude prior to thrusting rearward. The depth of this trough and its precise location both vary depending on the forward speed and rhythmic action of the whole body. These swimmers have remarked during pre-competition warm-ups that they have "found *it* again" (zeroed in on their personal ideal stroke) when they get a fleeting sensation of air on their heels when their feet are in the "catch" position. Having once enjoyed this for-them-successful sensation, they search it out.

All of the variables of breaststroke swimming influence the resultant wave patterns, but it is the use of the torso, the movements of the head, and the timing of the breaths, that are the most significant. If they are poor, either individually or in consort, the entire stroke suffers, even though the swimmer may test out as superior in both arms-only and legs-only swimming. The resourceful coach would do well to "wed" each of his breaststrokers to their own best wave patterns.

Freestyle waves
Broadly speaking, good freestylers can be divided into two main categories. There are "two-wave" freestylers who are usually, but not always, sprinters who use an arched-back, busy-kick style; and there are "three-wave" stylists who tend toward the head-lowered, body-stretched-out, subdued type of swimming seen more in "distance" events.

It would be wrong to categorically assume that of these styles one is right for sprinting while the other is best for distance events—especially now that the pace speeds of longer events are approaching the sprint speeds of not long ago. I have observed many world-class "three-wave" sprinters, and I have seen fine 1500s turned in by "two-wave" stylists.

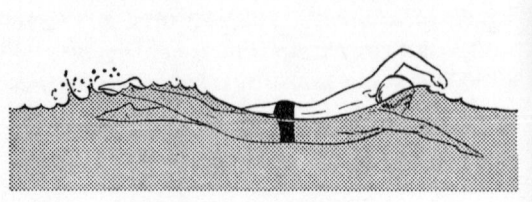

TWO-WAVE FREESTYLE

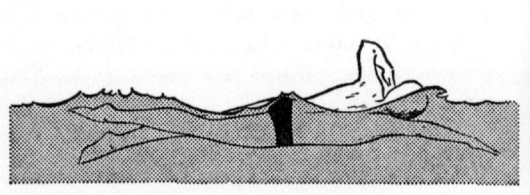

THREE-WAVE FREESTYLE

The two-wave freestyler, I am sure, is more dependent on how his style blends in with his waves than is his three-wave team mate. The two-wave swimmer, at speed, pushes up a higher bow wave. The trough that follows this wave is correspondingly broader and deeper. The second wave, which is influenced by the size of the first, rises high also and crests with its "V" coming away from about the midpoint of the lower legs. The whole arrangement sees the swimmer draped, or craddled, between the two waves as if lying belly-down in a hammock. In this position, and relying a lot on *feel* to maintain his wave-making shape, the swimmer "rides" along with the waves he creates.

I recall one of my swimmers in particular, Jane Hughes, who was not exceptional at either arms-only or legs-only but who "put it all together" nicely and was literally *wafted* along to two world-record certificates. (A definition of "waft" is: "to cause to move as if by the impulse of waves".) Her style depended on the total of her movements blending into the rise-and-fall-and-rise-again of the two waves she herself created.

The *classic* style of Don Schollander was a good example of two-wave freestyle—in fact it was at the 1964 Olympic Games, in which he starred, that I first recognized the wave-pattern phenomenon and its value as a coaching aid. The body bows downward in a swaybacked manner, the arms arch, elbows up, over the bow wave and utilize, to a degree, the piled-up water of this wave during the initial stages of each pull. From the waist rearward, the body is given impetus by the oncoming swell of the second wave. The swimmer's kicking action (which is usually steady and near the surface) serves to keep the legs well up in the water so as to facilitate what amounts to "body surfacing" on the part of the thighs and lower legs as they enjoy a downhill ride on the front side of the second wave.

I've noticed that those successful freestylers who are smaller of stature yet powerfully built through the shoulders are almost invariably two-wave swimmers. For them, the fitting of the body snugly into the trough between the two waves seems to be easier (which may explain, at least in part, why size is not the determining factor it is in many other sports).

As I've said, the two-wave style calls for a putting of it all together; the stroke must function as a whole. To me, this explains why it is so often unproductive when a coach or a swimmer attempts to copy and indiscriminately mix stroke components "lifted" from other swimmers. Some styles, and I am now including all four of the Fina-defined strokes, when they are copied, should be copied in their entirety or not at all!

The three-wave freestyler produces a lower bow wave. The second wave starts at about the hips, and the third vees outward from the midpoint of the lower leg (where the second wave of the two-wave pattern starts). The troughs are narrower and shallower. The swimmer spreads his length, from head through to just above the ankles, between the first and the third waves and maintains this arrangement as a matter of *feel*. He is usually taller and/or leaner—enjoying a favourable length-to-width ratio and less of his effort is expended in wave making.

I'll digress at this point to mention a fact or two about a related subject—ship design. Ships and boats are more efficient and smoother riding when their hulls are proportioned to fit into the wave patterns they create. Designers try to have the last wave crest near the stern. They know, for example, that a two-and-one-half wave arrangement isn't nearly as satisfactory as a pure two- or three-wave pattern. A boat-owning friend once told me of an instance in which a large pleasure boat was cut in two and lengthened without regard to the wave-pattern phenomena—an additional section was added to the middle. The boat, which had once been finely tuned became an uncomfortable clunker. In it's new form it was at odds with its own waves.

Many freestylers will, on occasion, shift abruptly from a three-wave to a two-wave pattern and back again as they move up and down the speed scale, passing through the uncomfortable in-between stages as quickly as possible. This also serves to further explain why so many of the best freestylers roll *abruptly* from a body position on the one side to a body position on the other: they *feel* the need to avoid the inefficient wave-pattern relationship of the central, lie-flat body position.

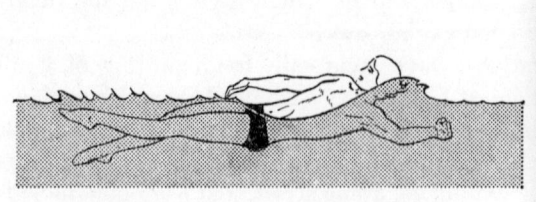

Backstroke waves
I think it's significant that a high percentage of the best backstrokers have naturally-rounded shoulders and upper backs, and that they tend to carry their heads well forward when standing. As mentioned in my backstroke chapter, the rounding and slouching forward of the shoulders, either naturally or contrived, sets the shoulder-girdle for a more efficient delivery of pull-push power. It's also instrumental in creating the distinctive bow wave common to most of the best backstrokers.

In a manner of speaking, it is a "chicken or the egg?" situation—I'm not sure which is more important; distinctive wave, or the improved set of the shoulder-girdle. It's academic, I suppose, for the two are intrinsically bound to each other. So much so, in fact, that the coach may use the wave patterns in checking on whether the set of the shoulders is right.

The "V" of this type of bow wave tends to be more bluntly shaped around the head and shoulders than is the case with the other strokes; it spreads more to either side. The head, neck, and rounded upper back are supported, pillow-like, as the back of the neck is driven relentlessly forward like the prow of a Viking ship. The shoulders take turns in rolling up high, high enough to clear the impeding water as they lead the arms up and over the water in each recovery.

A word of caution: Don't expect to see this type of well-defined wave when viewing your average backstroker. The ranks of good backstrokers being as sparse as they are, not many examples of this type of wave are to be seen outside of the best meets. Also, keep in mind that it is a phenomenon of fast swimming seen only when a select few "pour on speed".

The trough following this bow wave exposes the torso from the waist up. The second wave vees out from the sides of the hips. It is considerably lower and less-well defined than are its counterparts in the other strokes. Because of the generally deeper and more froth-producing nature of the kick in backstroke there is no third wave to speak of.

The "living bow wave" happens to be an important part of the backstroke I prefer. I look for it in my coaching. In particular, I look to see if the swimmer's hair is driven *forward, i.e. ahead* of the swimmer! This oddity was a reliable check when tuning up Elaine Tanner's world record form, and I've since noticed it with others, including Olympic and World Champion, Roland Matthes.

Butterfly waves
I've left this stroke to the last because its wave patterns are the most complex. They form and dissipate and reform again in time with the in-and-out rhythm of the stroke. During the breathing/arm-recovery phase, when the swimmer has his upper body at or above the surface, a bow wave is formed; but for good flyers this amounts to little more than a healthy ripple because the swimmer

is emerging from below rather than bulling his way along at the surface. The swimmer's momentum should carry his head and forward-swinging arms over and beyond this puny, temporary wave. Then the swimmer strikes undisturbed water with the characteristic and spectacular splashdown of the head, shoulders, and arms—in that order—as he reaches for the beginning of a new stroke. On doing so, a new, localized wave pattern is born only to be left behind as the swimmer's upper body temporarily abandons the surface and passes cleanly below this wave's leading edge to emerge yet again farther along. When the best flyers swim, only their hips remain constantly near enough to the surface to make steady wave patterns, but in the midst of the splashings, fore and aft, any waves they generate are insignificant.

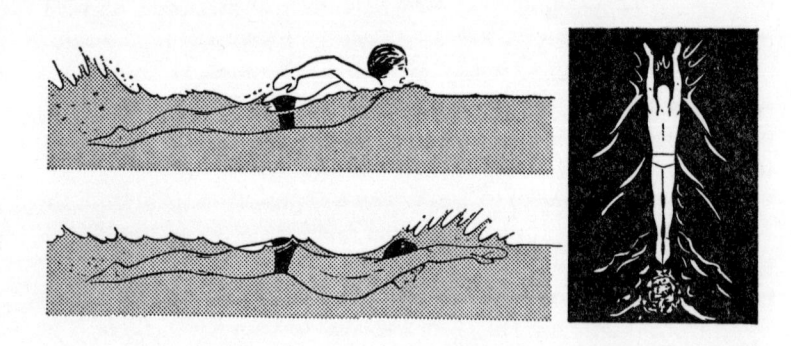

In assessing butterfly technique, I look for a washboard effect in the waves left behind the swimmer. The water seems to bounce in swells. Each downward slamming of the chest imparts to the water a force that rebounds upward under the thighs (the swimmer moves forward) giving the swimmer the sensation of being tossed along from wave to wave. The swimmer should consciously initiate this rhythm and then "stay with it", or "ride it out".

One thing is certain, it's only when a butterflyer swims fast that the water comes "alive" and assists him. For many years now, there have been coaches who have suggested that the stroke is easier at a reasonable speed—"flying speed", I call it—than at slow speeds. The water has its own minimum rate of responding. To utilize this phenomenon, and to practise the "true" stroke, I prefer my flyers to train only over distances they can successfully "ride out"; short distances at first, then, as their fitness improves, longer swims—but almost never do I give them "over distance" work. Also, I don't recommend arms-only butterfly in training, because of the "un-butterfly" waves it produces; better the swimmer should do full-stroke (and anyway, too many flyers neglect the use of their legs). Butterfly sprinters, in particular, should train mostly at sprint speed, using short, fast repeats, in order to master the use of their special, sprint-speed waves. It doesn't surprise me that so many flyers who are good at the 200 are only fair at the hundred; their stressing of mileage tends to preclude brilliant speed; for them, a 100 is a "short 200", but that isn't good enough, partly because of the difference in wave patterns.

Butterfly styles differ. The flexibility of the individual, his buoyancy, the type of arm entry he uses, the rhythm and force of his kicking—all of these will influence the nature of the waves he makes.

In summation

For too long, coaches have been blind to the behaviour of waves around their athletes. Wave patterns do not create themselves, they are a direct result of the swimmer's movements. Slight variations in the angle of the torso, the degree of roll, the entry of the arms, etc., can bring about profound changes for the better— or for the worse—in the effectiveness of a swimmer's technique, and such changes manifest themselves in the form of improved, or worsened, wave patterns.

In the over-arm strokes—free, back, and fly—the relative position of the first trough can be a guide in determining the best length of an individual's stroke. It is simply easier and more natural to withdraw the arms and hands from the water where it is lowest.

It goes without saying that it is easier to study the distinctive wave patterns of swimmers when the water is smooth to begin with, but, with practice, a discerning eye can isolate enough information of value even in a crowded workout session.

Wave patterns, and the fact that swimmers are inescapably "married" to them, can best be appreciated by the veteran coach who has never before given the matter much thought when he allows himself to bend over and look at things upside down, as described in Chapter 2. His swimmers will appear to be swimming across the ceiling, and the regularity of their wave patterns will fairly leap into focus.

A reader might get the impression that I believe it is waves that move swimmers magically to the other end of the pool. Obviously they can't. Work is involved as in any athletic endeavour. All I'm suggesting is that wave patterns can be a reliable guide to the efficiency of a technique, and that in some instances the swimmer actually realizes a return on his effort expended in wave making. As much as we would like to avoid making waves as we swim, our dimensions are such that we can't. So, if we can't escape making waves, we might as well make good ones—we might as well "go with the grain".

CHAPTER 7

Starts and Turns

A swimmer would protest vigorously if he were to find himself assigned to a lane which notches several feet into the deck area at the starting end. He simply wouldn't accept being asked to start from a yard or so behind the others or to swim that much farther per length. So why, in a fair race, will that swimmer accept the giving up of that same yardage at the start and at each turn? Any frequent spectator at swim meets has seen this happen many times.

Skill at starts and turns is reflected, one way or another, in the overall elapsed time of each individual in a race, and these days major events are timed to hundredths of a second, so intense is the competition. Clearly, starts and turns deserve more attention in training than they usually get.

On the average, a senior swimmer moves through the water at about six or seven inches per tenth of second—about a handlength per tenth of second. A single handlength, and often much less, can spell the difference between winning and coming, say, fourth, especially in a sprint. In a long course 1500-metre freestyle race that handlength difference can mount up to 2.9 seconds (29 turns); the same event in a 25-metre pool would produce a difference of 5.9 seconds (59 turns). When the loss is five handlengths a turn, the figures mount up to a shocking 14.5 and 29.5 seconds respectively—enough to eliminate a contestant from the final and perhaps from being allowed to enter at all.

In short, an event is not just a swimming race; it's a start-swimming-turning race. The contestant should think of it as a challenge such as: "I'm here to prove I can beat you at starting, swimming, and turning."

Diving starts
A century ago, in the 1870s, according to an encyclopedia of the period, the recommended "starting stance" for the racing dive was quaint indeed. It involved having one foot forward, toes curled over the "edge of the bath", or "mark"; the other foot was placed well to the rear; the body was turned sideways; both arms were pointed theatrically rearward, the forward arm across the chest; the head faced the water; (see illustration).

On the signal to start (perhaps the dropping of a hanky—borrowed from horse racing of the day) the swimmer flung himself upon the water and into the then-popular side-stroke.

In the years since then, many starting stances, some of them equally quaint, have been tried by individuals or adopted "in vogue" by swimmers of the succeeding eras. Some involved elaborate posturings and presumed mechanical (kinesiological) efficiency. World sprint record holder Gottvalles, of France, at the 1964 Olympic Games stood erect, arms overhead in the manner of an erectly standing chimpanzee, while waiting for the "gun". Through the mid-Fifties, many Australian stars bent over and clasped their hands loosely behind their backs, forearms resting on their buttocks, while waiting for the starting signal; their theory was that by exerting moderate parting tension on the clasped hands and then releasing the grip suddenly when the gun sounded, the hands and arms would spring around, mousetrap style, and get the swimmer moving sooner. It was, more than anything, a bad habit developed in training while waiting for a starting time on a pace clock. A number of the better-known swimmers used it, and as might be expected the lesser-lights copied it faithfully.

Wide stances, narrow stances, deep crouches, no crouch, winding-up of the arms, low trajectory, high trajectory, and many other variations too numerous to mention have been tried and tested, sometimes empirically, sometimes with a degree of scientific analysis thrown in. The search is still going on.

Until just after the Second World War, swimmers were not required to remain motionless while waiting for the final starting signal. Coaches and swimmers tried to gauge the cadence of the Starter's commands so as to still be in contact with the block when the gun was fired; this was known as the "rolling start". There was concern on the part of swimmers and coaches when the "remain motionless" rule came into force. It was felt that the old records, made with the rolling start, would never be broken. I recall a couple of heated arguments with officials who enforced the "new rule". (They were right, I was wrong; ironically, seven years later I was the Official Starter at the 1954 British Commonwealth Games.)

Not only has there been theorizing as to which is the best stance; divergent opinions have been offered in regard to the best path through the air and through the water leading to the first stroke. In the 1920s Johnny Weissmuller worked on landing as **flat as possible** *onto* (not into) the water. While in the air he raised one leg and the opposite arm higher than the rest of his body so as to be able to smack them down just as he hit the water; this was done to keep the whole of the body as shallow as possible for a torpedo-like slide along the surface as he furiously flutterkicked (at least that was the theory behind it). Others commenced the flutterkick (in freestyle races) while still in the air, presumably to "get their motor running" without delay (unwittingly, they paid the price of increased drag in the initial stages of the plunge through the water).

For a long time it was thought to be "obviously better" to try for as much distance as possible through the air—I used to tell my swimmers to pretend to be Tarzan lunging for a vine that's a little too far away, but try, and then "save yourself" and plunge cleanly into the water below.

In the Wind-Up Dive of today (see illustrations) the arms are

THE WIND-UP START

(1) On "Take Your Marks", the swimmer assumes the position shown, feet slightly apart and parallel to each other, toes curled over the "Mark", arms relaxed, body loose and ready to respond instantly. (2) On the "gun", the swimmer drops his shoulders and head (a common fault is to raise up, or stand up a little at this stage); note that the arms start *forward and upward* into their wind-up; note also that the toes instinctively come up; these actions combine to get the swimmer moving forward. (3) The wind-up continues as the knees bend more and the torso drops lower; the toes clamp down as the heels rise. (4) The arms have swung around in time to blend into, and add to, the animal-like lunge from the block. (5) The mass of the body is now forward of the block. (6) Out over the water the head rises instinctively, the swimmer looks to the far end of the pool, the arms stop suddenly in a diagonally downward position and action which transfers their independently developed momentum, gained in the wind-up, to the mass of the body, pulling it farther into the dive. (7) The head is lowered in time to join the streamlined-for-entry shape of the body.

(NOTE: This sequence is based on the dive of Steve Clark who was known for his superior starting ability; Clark recorded 52.9 for 100 metres in the 1964 Olympic Games to equal the World Record.)

swung *forward* upward, and over and around and then stopped before they reach the true "point" position; this abrupt stopping of the arm swing brings off what is known as "transfer of momentum". The inertia of the suddenly-stopped mass of the arms is transferred to the trunk of the body, thus increasing the forward momentum of the whole of the swimmer. Then just prior to the entry, the swimmer alters his body alignments by tucking his head down between his arms and by raising his hips and legs to form an arrow-like shape for a slightly angled-in entry *into* (not onto) the water. Only a few swimmers master this, but it is well worth the effort.

What I have described so far has pertained primarily to the freestyle start. For decades now breaststrokers have generally used a more lofting trajectory through the air—as if diving over a hurdle—and a shorter entry (entry point nearer the starting end). These swimmers, knowing they were going to utilize underwater swimming, have tried to enter the water at a steeper angle and with less splash than their freestyle team mates. Upon reaching their desired depth, they alter their path upward and continue to slip through the water parallel to the surface.

Eventually a few observant freestylers and coaches noticed that during group starting-practice sessions the breaststrokers were usually ahead of the more-spectacular, surface-splashing freestylers for a distance of up to eight metres, and this without their having done anything but pierce into and through the water. Richard Pound, of Canada, used this "breaststroke short entry" when he won the sprint freestyle at the 1962 British Commonwealth Games, defeating McGregor and other top-rated sprinters. Ten years later, Mark Spitz and a significant number of other swimmers put it to good use at the Munich Olympics; they went one further and married it to the relatively recent innovation known as the "grab start".

During the mid-Sixties a few—a very few—outstanding swimmers were experimenting with this new form of starting stance. The story heard most was that it was a special, remedial sort of thing for swimmers who were "too slow in their reflexes" and who were constantly being left behind at the "gun" when they used the conventional wind-up starts.

None of the swimmers in the sprint finals at the 1968 Olympic Games used the grab start although in the few years prior to

THE GRAB-START

(1) On "Take Your Marks", the swimmer steps forward and positions his feet, toes over the edge, and then bends down and lightly grasps the platform; some place their hands as shown, outside of the feet; others prefer to grasp the platform between their feet; some grasp the sides of the block. (2) On the "gun" the swimmer *grabs* hard and yanks his shoulders down, the head is swung down violently (the entire head goes lower than the level of the knees). NOTE that the hips remain high (squatting lower is a common fault). (3) Once off balance and committed to the dive, the hands release their hold and move forward into the dive (there is no attempt at a wind-up); NOTE that the head instinctively rises, adding to the surge of the dive. (4) The action continues into a panther-like lunge. (5) The flight of the body follows a curved path leading to a clean entry *into* the water. (6) The body glides into the water, piercing the surface with a minimum of splash, and prepares to alter course so as to move through the water below, and parallel to the surface.

those Games some girls had "gone under the minute" with it. In the main, the coaching pundits rejected the grab start, claiming that while it might get the swimmers moving sooner it lacked momentum and made the entry too short. But the best coaches aren't about to be behind the times for very long; at the 1972 NCAA (U.S. Collegiate) Championships every finalist in the 50- and 100-yard freestyle events used the grab start, and Mark Spitz used it in his spectacular butterfly swims.

Once the virtues of the short entry and submerged slide through the water are understood, the whole sequence from grab start stance, through to the taking of the first stroke, comes into focus.

The initial stance makes possible a very quick launching. The swimmer positions his feet carefully over the "mark". He reaches down and lightly grasps the starting platform with both hands. On the starting signal, he *grabs hard* and literally *yanks* his shoulders *downward* while at the same time driving his head low—the whole of his head should go lower than the level of the knees. This combined action, together with the keeping of the hips high (it's a common mistake to merely squat lower) tips the swimmer forward quickly to where his body is ahead of the starting block, the better to be driven forward into the dive. The action is so fast there is no time for a wind-up of the arms; the swimmer merely aims into the point position and concentrates on his angle of entry. Once below, he slides parallel to the surface. To come up stroking, he arches his back and pulls. Done well, the chances are that the dive sequence will bring him up into the race ahead of his more-conventional rivals. Even when the grab start is deficient in "grab"—as it is with perhaps four out of five swimmers I've observed—it is at least the equal of the average wind-up dive.

I want to stress that to merely not wind-up, and to merely rest one's fingers on the block, does not mean that the swimmer is using the grab start. The clue to the success of the initial movements of the start lies in the word "grab". A dictionary definition of "grab" is: "a sudden grasping action; to take hastily". So when waiting for the signal, the swimmer should simply prepare to grab; when the signal is given, he should react with a vigorous grabbing action. He should not, as so many do, merely release his hands and "sort of" dive in.

No matter which dive is used, the grab start or the wind-up

start, the swimmer should angle into the water, slide along below the surface and then come up. Done right, there will be a stretch of undisturbed surface between where he entered and where he returned to the surface.

The illustrations accompanying this chapter show the two most successful forms of the racing dive to date. Note that in both, the head and shoulders are brought downward suddenly and vigorously when the signal is given. A common fault, one that can cost valuable tenths of seconds, is to raise the head and shoulders—to stand up a little—instead of dropping them lower. This is one reason why the grab start, which at least uses the arms as restraining devices to prevent such rising, is faster.

I suggest that both forms of the dive be taught to swimmers. Whichever dive they use in serious competition should be the one in which they have the most complete confidence.

A good drill for getting the value of the wind-up across to those who wind-up the wrong way, or without "zip", is to have them take *three* wind-up revolutions, getting faster as they go, and then blend their lunge into the last part of the third full swing so as to have that swing add momentum to their dive.

Starts have tended to suffer since the widespread acceptance of swimming goggles; the esthetically satisfying sensations of the hard, clean plunge and the streamlined glide through the water that follows are rarely experienced by those who, in order not to dislodge their goggles, jump in or start from a push-off for all of their training swims. I suggest that swimmers experiment and find how best to hold their goggles in place, perhaps shifting the head-band higher, perhaps adding a second rubber band. Goggles have been worn successfully in major races, so the problem can be overcome.

When conditions are safe enough, I like to see swimmers take running dives in order to "live" that great feeling of plunging into and through the water. It's a good idea, also, to have pure sprint sessions of perhaps 15 to 20 minutes duration at least once or twice a week. The swimmers enjoy it, it's a good way to close off a "quality" workout. The swimmers should form up in sprint lines *on the deck*, and then with "called starts" (by the coach) they sprint single lengths, or widths (very good from time to time), with the second line starting perhaps five seconds after the first, and so on, climbing out (good for the muscles) at each end in order to do the next sprint *from a dive*. Most swimmers will discard their goggles for this routine, and that's good.

Backstroke starts

In spite of its apparent simplicity, there are a number of facets and variations of the international backstroke start that are not well known even to veteran coaches.

Starting blocks and their handgrips vary considerably from pool to pool, and so does the texture and slipperiness of the end walls. The wise swimmer will therefore do some practice starts, preferably in the lane which will be his, during the pre-meet warm-up period. He will search out the best positions for his hands and feet.

All too often only one set of handgrips are provided and usually they are fixed at a height suitable only for senior males and the taller of the senior females. They impose an unreasonable hardship on smaller girls and on the vast majority of age groupers, yet invariably there are more of the latter than there are senior-class swimmers who will use the pool during its life. There is every reason for having a choice of handgrips, high, medium, and low, and no reason for not having such an arrangement. Those who control the sport should look into this problem. No swimmer should be expected to dangle awkwardly from handgrips that are too high.

Many swimmers, especially girls, prefer to grasp the overflow gutter (when there is one). World records have been set starting from such a low placement of the hands.

Most backstrokers position their feet with one near the surface (but paying heed to the Rule requiring that the toes be under water and not curled over the gutter), the toes of the other foot being just below the level of the heel of the topmost foot. This arrangement lessens the chance of slipping; it also allows for better control of the spring from the wall. One leg lifts the swimmer then both push him away from the wall.

On "Take Your Marks" the swimmer draws himself as close to the starting block as he can, and lifts himself partly out of the water. I've seen a swimmer turn his head to the side in order to get his nose out of the way—that's the kind of "close" I'm speaking of here. This in-close position precludes a further drawing inward when the gun sounds and thus saves about half a second.

THE BACKSTROKE START

(1) The swimmer waits at the ready with one foot positioned higher than the other. (2) On "Take Your Marks", the swimmer pulls himself inward and upward toward the block. (3) On the "gun" he uses his *arms* and his legs to lift himself almost straight up, clearing his buttocks from the water. (4) He springs backward, swinging his arms around low over the water; note that the head is tilted back. (5) The lunge continues, the feet never quite clearing the water, but with most of the body in the air in a position like that of a backward "swan dive". (6) Just prior to striking the water, the swimmer raises his head and smacks the back of his neck and the region between his shoulder blades flat on the water—the swimmer should experience this smacking sensation—as his body lands stretched out on the water. (7) The swimmer finds himself below the surface, arms stretched out in front, as he commences to kick; the length of the run below the surface will vary with the swimmer's kicking and streamlining abilities.

On the starting signal the swimmer consciously lifts himself *straight up* and then he pushes away *with his hands and arms* as well as with his feet and legs; it's a mistake to merely let go of the handgrips.

The flight over the water should resemble an upside-down "swan dive". The arms should sweep around to their point position through the horizontal plane. When they are flung over the top, the tendency is to arch the body too much which usually results in steering the swimmer too deep into the water. Another trick for avoiding going too deep is to hold the head up, chin near the chest, at the moment of impact; this makes for a straighter body-shape throughout.

A little-known refinement is to land slightly on one's side; this arrangement helps the swimmer to split the water with less drag than he would encounter were he to be dead-level flat (you'll recall my discussing this water-splitting advantage of the body on its side at the surface in my freestyle chapter).

After the entry the swimmer should stretch himself to his straightest alignment, and then when he has moved perhaps his own body-length while submerged he should start to kick. The swimmer pulls *with one arm* while the other remains on duty, so to speak, as an integral part of the streamlined body. The first pull should be timed so that that arm is able to go smoothly into its recovery through the air.

So far I have discussed the start sequence which is the most commonly seen today; it has changed hardly at all from that used by the stars of twenty years ago. There is, however, another, basically different, style that should be better known; I say that because it might be the answer for certain individuals. I refer to the start used so successfully by the great South African world record holders, Karen Muir (the youngest swimmer ever to hold a world record) and Ann Fairlie.

When at the ready, waiting for the starter's command, there was nothing unusual about their position, but on "Take Your Marks" they *sank* lower in the water, until their shoulders were awash. On the starting signal they pushed up and then away, out of their low position—rather like a missile fired from a submarine. Their arm-swing and entry were no different. It was a strange sight at the 1966 U.S. Championships to see the two of them, side by side in the middle lanes, go *down* when all the others climbed higher on hearing the starter's command. They lost nothing on the start, and I suspect that their arms—which had been excused the straining labour of holding their bodies high—were able to function better right from the first stroke of the swim.

In the United States (and perhaps in some other countries) a third form of start is allowed *in short course competition*. The rules-makers in the U.S. reasoned that since times made in short course pools (25-yard and 25-metre pools, for example) are not recognized by the international swimming association there is nothing to prevent a nation from having slightly different rules for competitions in such pools. They decided to allow backstrokers to have their toes in the gutter—or to even stand in the gutter—*in short course pools* only. The danger of slipping is virtually eliminated, and all have the same advantage. For a while, some elaborate posturings were common, but now, after much trial-and-erroring, the best U.S. backstrokers, when "swimming short course", use a start that differs from the international start only in that the toes of both feet are placed over the lip of the gutter. In this "special rules" start, it is especially important that the swimmer draw himself up tight to the block.

Relay take-overs
Even at the world level relay relief take-overs are seldom done well, yet they are often the deciding factor in the outcome of close races. In dual meets, when relay teams score higher than individuals, this skill becomes especially important.

Literally, the relay exchange calls for good teamwork. The incoming swimmer must do his part and speed up his final lunge to the wall, even if it means distorting his stroke (keeping within the Rules). He must do his full part and "save" the exchange from disqualification.

The departing swimmer does not wait to see his team mate touch. Instead, he gauges the speed of the incoming swimmer, perhaps sinking gradually into his starting crouch in time with the approach of his team mate. When he is sure that his team mate can touch in time, he goes into his wind-up so as to be well into his dive sequence but with his toes still in contact with the block when his partner touches.

There is no point in using the grab start in a relay take-over because quickness in getting out of a dead-still position is not a

STARTS AND TURNS

factor. Better to use a wind-up start and get as much momentum as possible to carry one's self well out over one's team mate.

Relay members should practise in the order they will swim so as to learn how to save time, also they must become confident in their partners.

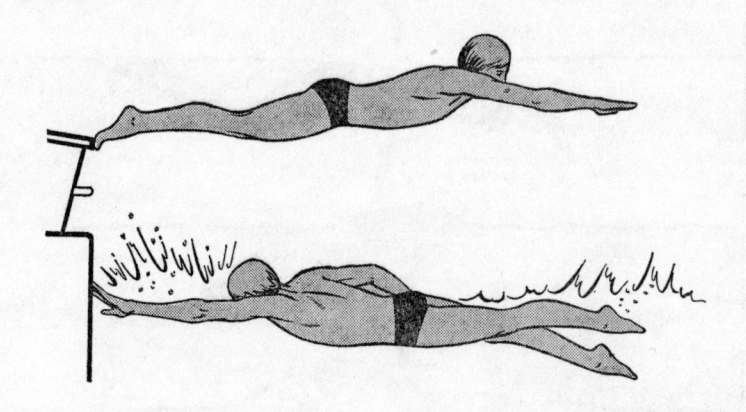

A good drill is to have the team line up in order at the block. The first swimmer dives and swims a few strokes, he then turns and swims back at top speed to "touch out"; the second swimmer dives directly over him and swims out a few strokes, turns and swims back in hard; and so on.

On turns in general

The only reason we turn in swimming races is so that we can use our lane over again. Obviously we don't want to waste time in reversing our direction, and if possible we want our turns to give us an advantage over our rivals. Turns are not done to be "flashy"; there are no merit points awarded for, say, doing a "flip" turn.

The Rules of freestyle require only that the swimmer touch the end wall with some part of himself to prove he has travelled the full distance of the length. The *free*-styler is permitted to move feet-first if he chooses, so in 1965 the old hand-touch was dropped. (One wonders why it was ever a rule in the first place.)

But it was retained in the so-called "form strokes" (backstroke, breaststroke, and butterfly) as a means of checking that swimmers travel the *full* distance, down to the last centimetre, according to "form", *i.e.* according to the Rules of these strokes.

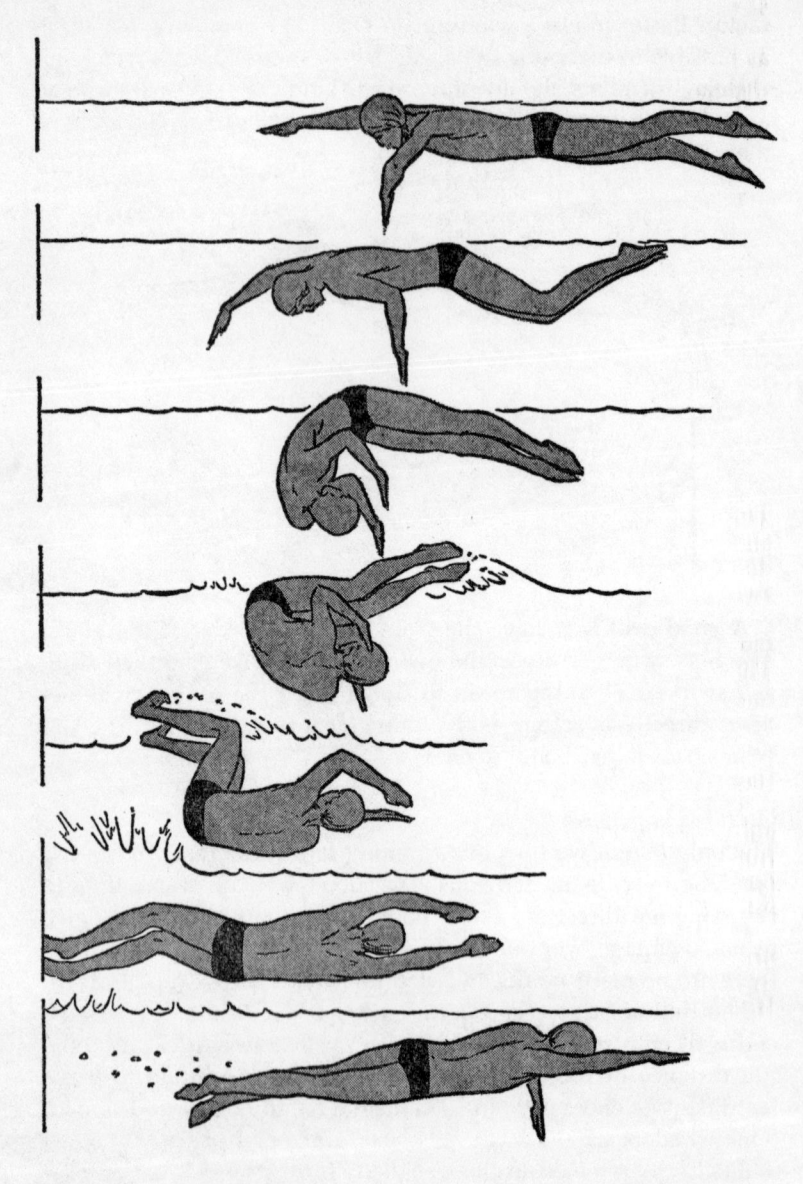

Freestyle tumble-turn
To use an "open turn" these days (with the head up, breathing, during the turn) brands a swimmer as a "rookie". There is no

excuse for even the youngest age grouper to use anything other than the aptly-named tumble turn.

The manoeuvre is basically a forward one-half somersault that becomes a "cartwheel". A pure one-half somersault would land the swimmer on his back for the push-off, so to save time the swimmer rolls on his side as he somersaults/cartwheels. His feet jam down hard pointing sideways one above the other. The push-off, which is immediate, starts with the swimmer on his side. He further rights himself as he moves away from the wall in the push-off.

Study the illustrated sequence carefully. Note that the swimmer does not come in too close. The bend at the knees when the toes and balls of the feet jam against the wall is about that of a basketball centre-forward prior to jumping for the ball. Note the action of the hands and arms. Some have presumed that the forearms should rotate the hands, palms toward the turning wall, for better scooping, but I have noticed that many swimmers, who are on high-mileage training programmes necessitating countless routine turns in training (especially when training in short-course pools), have evolved a scooping manoeuvre with the *backs* of their hands. It is just as effective, and certainly simpler.

The first stroke after a turn should be taken with the topmost arm. This, too, is something the high-mileage trainers evolved quite instinctively. Now that the speeds of freestyle are nearly the speed of the push-off, there is no point in trying for a prolonged glide out from the wall. The swimmer virtually rebounds from the wall directly into his stroke.

Perhaps the best way to teach this turn is to have the swimmer start from a standing position some seven metres out and with his arms at his sides dolphin kick himself toward the wall. As he comes within turning distance he exaggerates the downward thrust of his upper body in the last undulation and goes into a somersault. The chances are he will instinctively do all the right things with his head, arms, and legs to assist himself through the movements of the turn. The dolphin action of the legs at the start of the somersault is crucial. The driving of the head and shoulders down and under provides momentum for the somersault. The hands and forearms should perform as blades to assist the action by scooping and sculling.

Clearly, if one can't perform a satisfactory somersault in water one will have trouble learning the turn. Somersault drills, designed to familiarize swimmers with the sensations of flipping themselves over, therefore have a place in coaching. Here are a few:

The "magic circle": In waist-deep water the group stands in a large circle facing inward. One swimmer starts the group into action by leaping upward, somersaulting forward, and landing on his feet, holding his arms upward. A split-second after the first swimmer starts his movement, the swimmer next to him on one side starts his leap upward into a somersault. And so on around the circle, swimmer by swimmer, over and over again, getting faster and faster. This will instantly reveal which swimmers have trouble somersaulting. It also allows each swimmer to take his mind off his personal apprehension about being upside-down, etc. The swimmers should be prohibited from holding their noses. They should be forced to learn how to breathe out, keeping their nasal passages clear of water, while somersaulting.

Somersaults on the move: The swimmers swim a given distance of, say, 200 metres doing freestyle. On every fifth arm stroke they do a complete somersault and continue on: Left, right, left, right, left, *somersault*, right, left, and so on.

One in the middle, one at the wall: Swim crossways in the pool and do a complete somersault at the mid-point of each width and then do a true tumble turn at each wall. In wider pools, do two somersaults (separated by a few strokes) in each width plus the tumble turns at the walls. This is a good sprint drill when racing lines of swimmers start together from a dive; these lines may be composed of twenty or more swimmers, all starting together, depending on the length of the pool; there may be several flights of swimmers, each flight starting from a called start and swimming, say, four widths. It also works well when done relay fashion, widths or lengths. Invariably there will be some novice who will evoke laughter by losing his sense of direction when somersaulting.

The imaginative coach may come up with variations of his own. The ultimate answer, of course, is to insist that swimmers do a proper tumble turn *at every turn* in the course of their training swims.

STARTS AND TURNS

The "Magic Circle" is fun. Seniors as well as youngsters enjoy it, in fact one of my senior groups gave it its name.

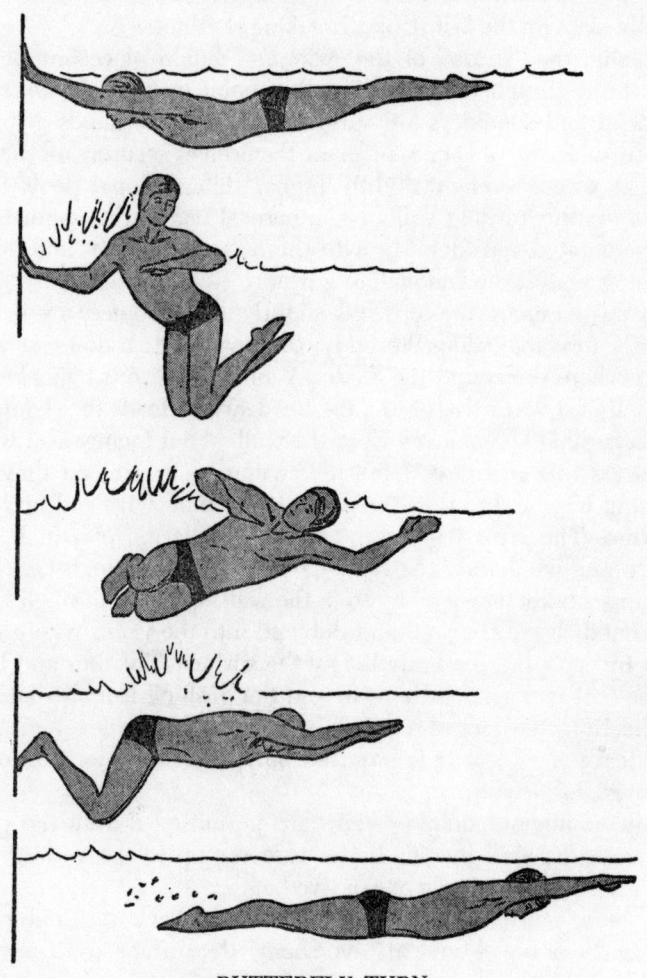

BUTTERFLY TURN

The butterfly turn
The basic turn is simple. There are, however, a few tips that may help.

The veteran swimmer will begin preparing for the turn several strokes out. He will either shorten or lengthen each of his last few strokes a little so that it works out that his hands will be ready in front when needed for the touch. It is "amateurish" indeed to have to glide into the wall dolphin kicking, or to come in awkwardly close on the last stroke, breaking rhythm.

Ideally, the "stride" of the swimmer should place him at the wall, arms stretched forward, at that point in his cadence when his head and shoulders are surging upward. The hands grip the gutter (when there is one) or plant themselves securely on the flat wall at water level or slightly higher (international pools have flat, no-gutter turning walls). The natural rise of the upper torso is exaggerated considerably with the help of the arms and hands pressing against the end wall or gutter.

As this happens, the hips sink slightly and the knees are drawn smartly forward below the body, the lower legs trailing, relaxed and perhaps crossed at the ankles. While the torso is being raised to an almost vertical attitude, the head swiftly leads the shoulders into a turning action away from the wall, about facing, as it were. To stress this swiftness, I tell my swimmers to pretend they are wearing wigs and to turn the head so fast their wigs end up back to front. The arms join in and speed up the movement. It is a pendulum-like action, the hips and legs swing through below as the upper body moves away from the wall, spinning through 180°. The hands leave the wall and descend into the water where they help by scooping the body below the surface. The toes and balls of the feet jam against the wall and the push-off is immediate.

The Rules no longer require the swimmer to be level once his toes leave the wall. It is required only that he be level prior to initiating his first stroke.

Any number of dolphin kicks are permitted during the glide out from the wall but it's better to come up to the surface and into the stroke after only one or two kicks.

It's wise not to breathe on the first stroke because if one plans to breathe one will tend to "overshoot" the surface and come too high through the surface to ensure getting air and not a mouthful of water. It will then take a few strokes to settle down into the best stroking rhythm.

The butterfly tumble turn
The Rules permit a tumble turn—provided the hands touch the turning wall properly—and it can be faster than the open turn,

but it demands a high degree of "rag-doll" flexibility of the shoulders. Swimmers should not attempt it in serious competition until they have it mastered.

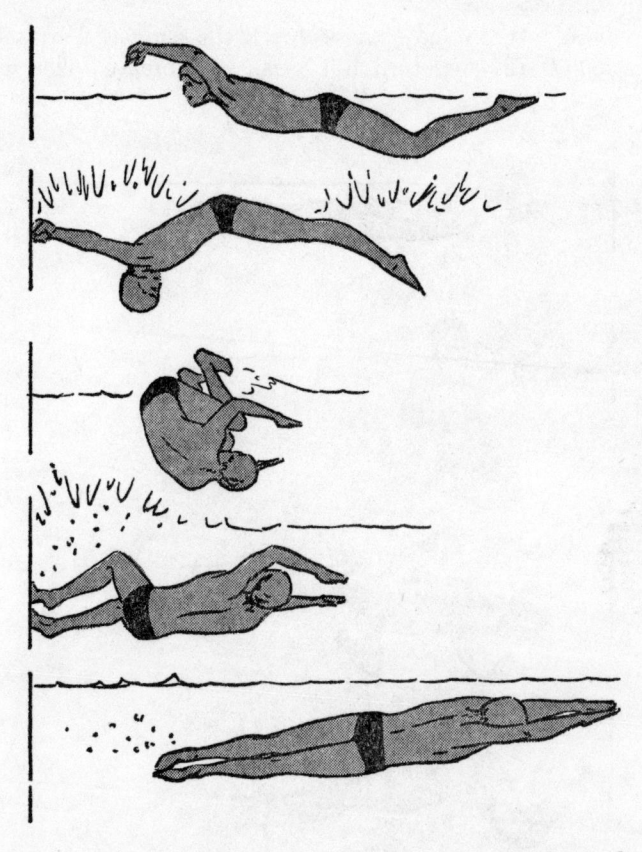

The trick is to have the arms and hands spread wide on the last arm entry. This allows the swimmer to start into his straight-over-the-top somersault *before* the hands touch the wall. Once the touch is made—and the touch should be light, but legal—the hands knife away from the wall to assume their role as spear points for the shove-off. The swimmer spirals and rights himself as he darts, streamlined, toward his first pull.

This turn deprives the swimmer of the opportunity to take a big breath as he turns, which may require him to breathe on the first stroke. This turn also robs the swimmer of his chance to "survey the field" while pivoting his head high, which the basic "open" turn affords.

The breaststroke turn
The actual "turn around" manoeuvre is the same as that used in the basic butterfly open turn, but because the breaststroker, while

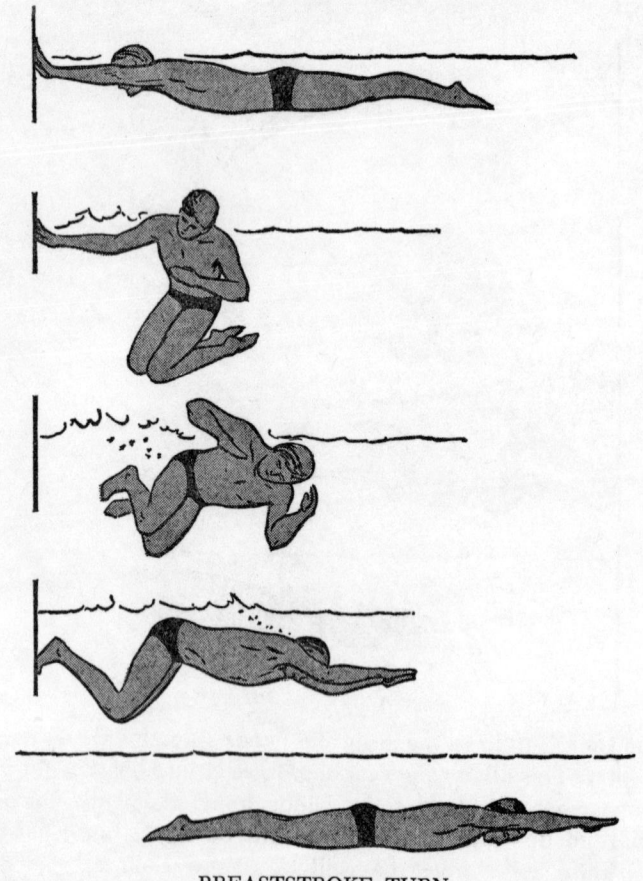

BREASTSTROKE TURN

turning, is also preparing for his underwater "pull-out" sequence, he should duck more abruptly downward than in the case of butterfly turning.

The action is, therefore, a turn and a duck dive. It reminds me of the swirling turn and dive sequence used so fluidly by seals and other aquatic animals when they swim back and forth in the familiar confines of their marineland tanks. Done well, this breaststroke "turn and submerge" action even creates the same sounds and swirls.

The breaststroker must be level as his toes leave the wall. His shove-off depth should be about two feet (for seniors); this depth works to his advantage in reducing drag. As he glides from the wall, at depth, he does nothing for a while except spear along cleanly. Then, when he feels himself slowing, he uses his arms simultaneously in a wide, powerful, round-the-side sweep to drive himself forward head first. By pulling around the side, in the horizontal plane, he lessens his chances of altering his level (constant depth) path through the water, and he minimizes the error of jackknifing his body, which would create additional drag, during the final stages of the pull-push. The arm sweep of this submerged pull resembles an exaggeratedly wide "keyhole pull" borrowed from butterfly, except that the final thrust is straight back to full extension. At the end of this pull-push the best swimmers consciously fuse their arms tightly to the body and scrunch their shoulders forward close to their ears, as if to compact themselves the better to pass through the porthole of a sunken ship (I tell my swimmers the porthole is jagged and rusty, so be extra compact and line up the body carefully).

Now, when the swimmer feels himself slowing again, he moves his hands forward cleanly close to the body and then forward into the point position. When the hands are nearly all the way forward he draws up his legs and breaststroke kicks himself *forward at the same depth*! This last is most important. Most so-called "good" breaststrokers fail in that they use this kick as a feeble means of getting themselves back to the surface. The great breaststrokers use this kick to drive themselves *still farther forward at the same depth*.

To surface, the swimmer arches his back and directs the plane-like hands upward. I have found, as a result of countless clockings, that it is a mistake to return gradually to the surface, with the "decks awash", as it were, like a movie submarine. It is much faster to alter course upward sharply. The drag factor is reduced, and the swimmer's buoyancy actually assists him to pop forward and upward into his surface swimming, like a submerged wood plank scooting to, and through, the surface.

This underwater breaststroke pull-out stroke sequence applies to the dive as well as the turn. With practice, it's not unusual for a swimmer to surface five or six of his bodylengths down the pool after a dive, after a turn perhaps four or five, but less when sprinting.

Many novices use their arms far too soon after diving or turning. I suspect they panic a little. Perhaps they think to themselves: "I'm in a race and I'm not *doing* anything." They have trouble reconciling the momentum-charged streamlined glide as being part of a very physical activity.

In teaching this pull-out sequence I like to have my swimmers swim crossways in the pool so they can gauge their movement by the lane markings on the bottom. They can then better appreciate that they are indeed speeding forward although they are not working.

I sometimes ask them to pretend they are each a swimming gadget developed by the Navy. After a dive or a turn they are *programmed* to hold the streamlined shape for a while, thus: Tick, tick, tick (for several seconds, or until they pass over two or three lines on the bottom), *pling*, *whirr*, *PULL!*, tick, tick, etc. (for several more seconds), tick, tick, arms go forward, *pling*, *whirr*, *KICK!*, tick, tick, etc., all of this explained with animated *gusto* on the part of the coach. I get good results with such stories.

Backstroke turns (general)
I've left backstroke turns to the last (of the "stroke" turns) because they are beset with a couple of unique problems. On his back, the swimmer is likely to be handicapped in judging his distance from the turning wall; and he must learn what amounts to two turns, a right-hand turn and a left-hand turn. (In the other strokes there is nothing to prevent a swimmer from always turning in the same direction.)

This means that during the approach to the wall the swimmer should collect his thoughts and organize his strategy. The Rules require a line of turn-warning pennants above the pool five metres (or yards) out from the end. Some coaches put store in the counting of strokes from the pennants to the wall, with the turn to be done "blind", as it were (the wall must be *here!*). I've found this precarious at best. I stress that my swimmers *know* for a fact where the end wall is. They are encouraged to take a "look see" around—even two look-sees—to establish this, especially when they are in a strange pool. This need not interfere with their stroking. It need not slow them at all. If anything, *it allows them to speed up* because of their extra confidence as they swim right into the turn, utilizing their forward momentum to help them in the execution of the turn itself.

The backstroke "spin" (or "whip") turn
This is still the standard turn used by Olympic Champions and world record holders.

It is a *turn* and *not* a "flip". The swimmer drops his recovering hand in beyond the centre-line, in line with its opposite shoulder. He arches his back and tilts his face back and down below the surface. His hand and arm absorb the shock of encountering the wall, and, like the trapped tip of a pole vaulter's pole, starts the swimmer through the misnamed "flip". The knees are lifted out as the heels are drawn toward the buttocks and then out of water. This smooth, coordinated action continues as the shock-absorbing arm now reacts by driving the head and shoulders down and around, away from the touching hand. (If the touch is made with the right hand, the head and shoulders go around to the left, and vice versa—it's a common mistake to cross this up and turn in the wrong direction, although I have seen some who should be left alone in their error because through practice it has become ingrained.) The onrushing, momentum-charged hips and now-elevated legs are whipped *around*, in a semi-cartwheel manner over the water. The non-touching arm aids by scooping and aiming the head towards its return trip down the lane. The feet are slammed down and the toes and the balls of the feet are jammed against the wall at a point level with, or slightly lower than, the average depth of the swimmer. The push-off is immediate. During this manoeuvre, the hands have positioned themselves near the sides of the head, ready to blend into the shove-off.

The whole of the turn reminds me of the lifting of a boom of a crane (the legs) out of water, swinging it (them) around (180°) above water (so as to escape drag) and then putting it (them) in again.

If the shove-off is too deep the problem is that the feet are jammed against the wall too high (if you push-off from the ceiling you go downward). Better to sink them a split-second farther down the wall, until the desired trajectory is achieved.

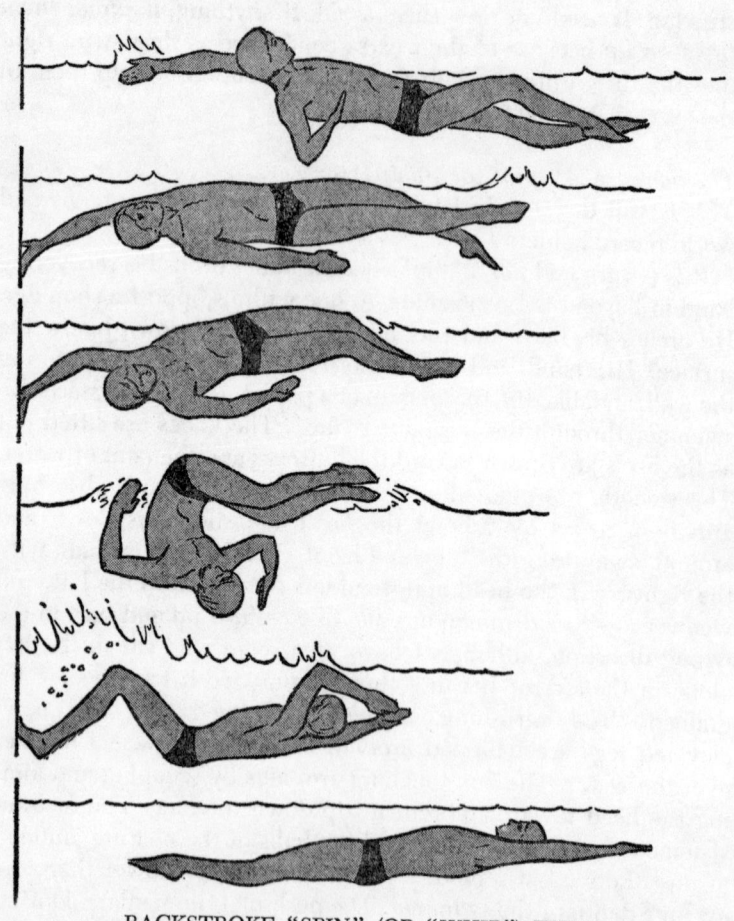

BACKSTROKE "SPIN" (OR "WHIP") TURN

This turn cannot be done properly at slow-motion speeds. It must be a quick lift of the legs and then, before the mass of the body can sink, a quick swing around of the legs. The head must go under. With practice, it is usual for a swimmer to introduce a semi-cartwheel movement.

The easiest way to practise this turn is to start from several metres out and on the back simply flutterkick in toward the wall while one arm is ahead pointing the way. In this manner the swimmer knows which hand will make the touch, so he can work on improving his weaker turning side.

It is good practice, also, to swim widths beginning each new width with a different arm making the first pull. This delivers the swimmer to the next turn with a different arm each time. Thus he can practise turning both ways.

In addition, I suggest that backstrokers practise their turns in mid-pool. They will then learn how to use the hands as scoops and they will learn how best to shift their weight around, legs over the water.

The backstroke "suicide" turn

This turn has a greater element of risk of disqualification, hence its bizarre name. It is, however, a very fast and comfortable manoeuvre.

It is nothing more than a roll-over (or more aptly a roll-*under*) into the prone position smoothly blended into a forward, freestyle-like, somersault. The swimmer finds himself quickly and solidly positioned on the wall for an ideal backstroke push-off.

The hazard is that the swimmer, if his judgement is off, may roll over beyond the allowed 90° vertical toward his breast *before* his hand touches the end wall.

The initial learning of this turn is best done away from a wall. The swimmer kicks along on his back, one arm in front, the other at his side. He then rolls *toward the arm at his side* over onto his breast. He then does a forward somersault. It's that simple.

Obviously, a swimmer should not attempt this turn in competition until he can do it consistently within the Rules. It is worth noting that this turn is not used by Roland Matthes.

The turns of the individual medley

A common weakness in individual medley swimming is to doddle for the first several strokes of each new stroke-leg. It's natural to be relieved, and to relax, as each stroke-leg is completed. The crafty competitor uses this knowledge and gains on his rivals at such times. He blasts off into each new stroke-leg of the race.

When switching from butterfly to backstroke the simplest turn is one which sees the swimmer touching with forward-stretched hands to jolt his upper body backward as he draws his bent legs through, pendulum style. This is followed by a short, shallow, and *fast* push-off into high-revving backstroke.

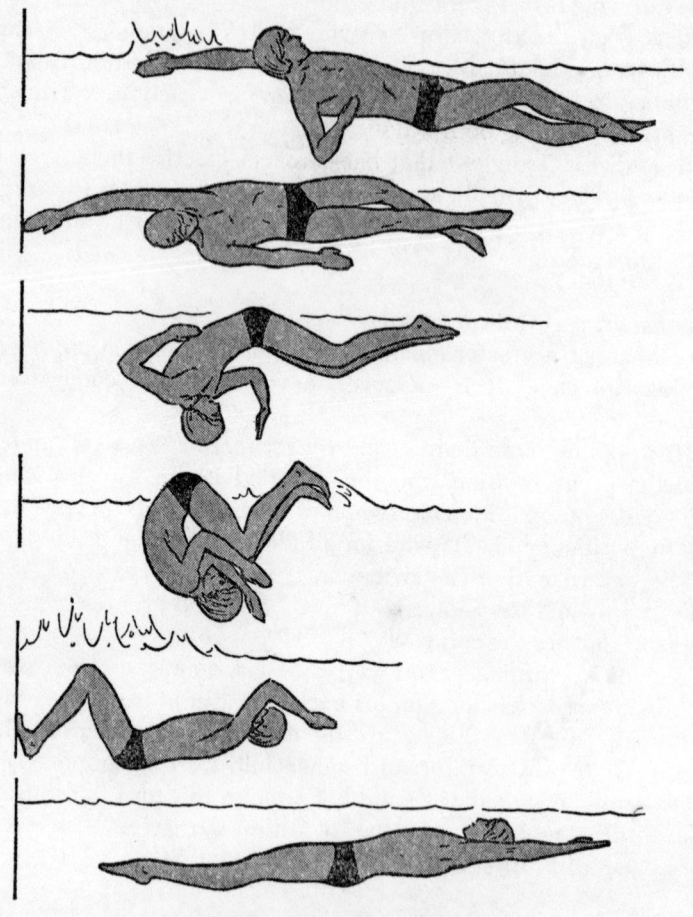

BACKSTROKE "SUICIDE" TURN

A variant used by some, which is claimed to be faster by as much as half a second, has the swimmer grab the gutter, or grips, and then execute a true backstroke start from a full crouch, just as if it were the beginning of a straight backstroke event.

Some of today's best medley swimmers do a straight-over-the-top somersault rather like the butterfly tumble turn described earlier. The only difference is that they stay on their back for the push-off. It is not a difficult manoeuvre, but it does cost a lost chance to breathe, and in an endurance event like the individual medley, especially at the end of the butterfly leg, that can be a hardship.

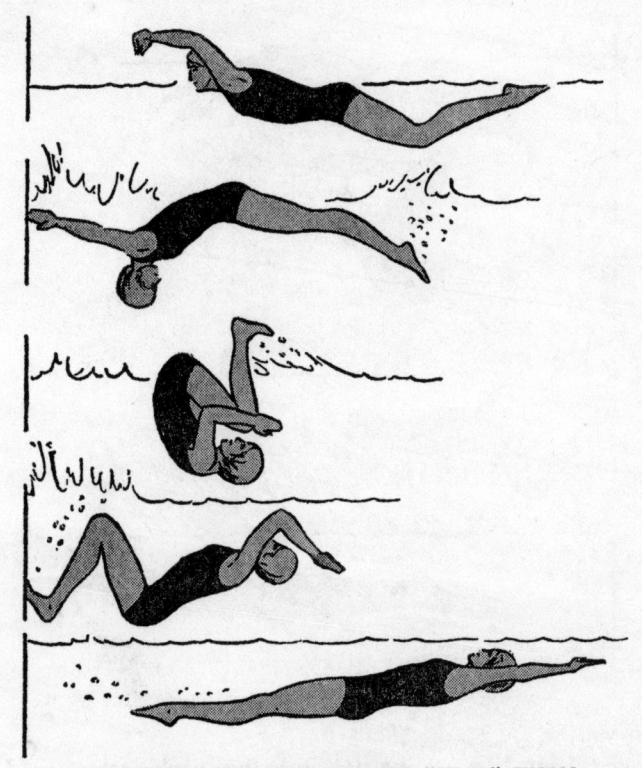

BUTTERFLY TO BACKSTROKE "FLIP" TURN

At the end of the backstroke leg some do a simple open turn, but the trend is to execute a backward flip onto the breast for the push-off. Some lay both hands back over their heads the better to execute this movement. Worth noting is that even world record breaststrokers will sometimes forego the breaststroke underwater "pull-out" and instead come up immediately swimming *and breathing*.

From breaststroke to freestyle the turn is simple and needs no description here. There is, however, a little trick, most swimmers will use freestyle armstrokes that are far too short for the first 20 metres or so of their freestyle leg; this is because they have come off breaststroke which uses short pulling actions. To correct this, I ask my medley swimmers to consciously stretch out their freestyle stroke as they begin that leg of the race.

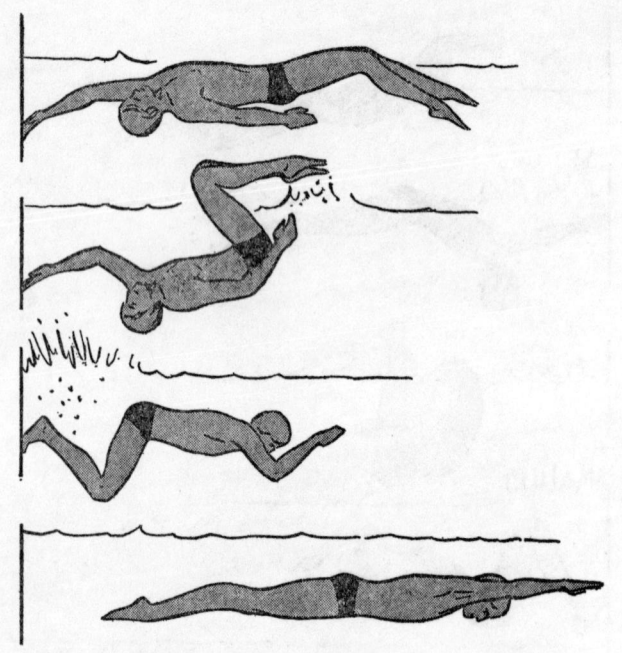

BACKSTROKE TO BREASTSTROKE "FLIP" TURN

In summation
Skill at starting and turning demands the coach's attention. I like to "tailor" these all-important adjuncts to the sport to each individual. What works for one doesn't necessarily work for another. I recommend using a stopwatch to time swimmers in special starts-and-turns sessions. I'll clock them from a dive out to some ten or twelve metres—to a point even with a deck drain, a crack in the deck, a guard stand, or whatever; it doesn't matter what the precise distance is, as long as it is the same all the time. Through trial and error, altering depths and stroke-sequence details, etc., it's possible to arrive at the best arrangement for each swimmer.

For turns, I use the same sort of procedures but I time them from, say, five metres out, through the turn, and back to the same point. They start their full-speed swimming farther out in the pool, of course. I start or stop my watch as they pass the reference point.

I've found that some breaststrokers are better off to forego the underwater pull-out and instead come directly to the surface after a dive or a turn. Similarly, in other strokes there are some who should glide farther than others, kick sooner, etc. Sometimes the unorthodox can pay off, there are some who *gain* on the backstroke push-off *by not kicking* at all until they start their first stroke. Recent star, Susan Atwood, of the U.S.A., did this instinctively (her coach, Jim Montrella, told me he didn't teach it to her). It looked like an inverted breaststroke shove-off and glide. When I tried it on my swimmers some adopted it while others did not. The stopwatch was the final arbiter.